Driving a Tandem

Off to the Olympic games? (M. Berthélémy)

Driving a Tandem

Paul Doliveux

J. A. Allen
London

British Library Cataloguing in Publication Data
A catalogue record for this book is available from the British Library.

ISBN 0. 85131. 674. 3

Published in Great Britain in 1996 by

J. A. Allen & Company Limited
1 Lower Grosvenor Place, London SW1W 0EL

© J. A. Allen & Company Limited 1996

No part of this book may be reproduced or transmitted in any way or by any means, electronic or mechanical, including photocopy, recording, or any information storage and retrieval system, without permission in writing from the publishers. All rights reserved.

Editor Elizabeth O'Beirne-Ranelagh
Designer Nancy Lawrence

Typeset by Setrite Typesetters Ltd; Hong Kong,
Printed by Dah Hua Printing Press Co. Ltd, Hong Kong

Dedication

To HRH Prince Philip, Duke of Edinburgh, with my courteous respects.

To Sallie Walrond LHHI with my great admiration.

To Tom Coombs avec mes bonnes amitiés et mes remerciements.

To Pierre de Chézelles, chairman of l'Association Française d'Attelage, and to Paul de Brantes, vice-chairman, who urged me to publish this book in English.

To Claudie and our three sons, Jerome, Christophe and Roch.

To Michel Berthélémy, my talented draughtsman relative – thank you, old chap!

My wife Claudie with our son, Roch.

'Going to the meet'. (Private collection)

Contents

Acknowledgements   x
Foreword *by Major Tom Coombs*   xi
Introduction   xiii

1. **Traditional English tandem driving**   1
   What is a tandem?   1
   Tandem driving through the years   1

2. **My favourite horses and ponies for a tandem team**   5
   English, American and French trotters   5
   Lusitanos and high-school dressage horses   7
   Pony tandems   10

3. **Tandem carts and carriages**   16

4. **Tandem harness**   20
   Traditional English harness   20
   Harness for both horses   20
   The harness of the wheeler   22
   The harness of the leader   23
   Accessories for a tandem equipage   24

5. **Putting to and moving off**   27
   Driving halters   27
   Putting the wheeler to a two-wheeled carriage in countries where one drives on the left   27
   Putting the leader into position in countries where one drives on the left   28
   Moving off in my own country, where one drives on the right   28

6. **The schooling of tandem horses**   29
   Terminology   29
   A dialogue between the driver and the tandem team   30
   The circus tradition   32
   The whip and the reflex response   32
   Handling the tandem whip   33

7. **Dressage schooling on the lunge**   39
   Lungeing equipment   40
   The benefits of lungeing the tandem horse   41
   Work on the long lunge line   41
   Work on the half-length lunge   46
   Work on the short lunge   51
   Conclusion   51

8. **Schooling the horse – other methods** 52
    Training the horse in long-reins 52
    Schooling the ridden horse 55
    Schooling the driven horse in single harness 56
    Epilogue 58

9. **Driving tandems** 59
    English tandem driving 59
    How to turn two horses in line to the left 60
    Holding English reins 60
    Using the English rein hold 62
    The varying positions of the driver's hands 63
    Changing direction 65
    Turning at a right angle 66
    Turning a corner in right-hand drive 68
    Playing the harp! 69
    Turning an acute angle at walk 70
    Putting theory into practice 73
    Driving on the road 73
    The wisdom of C. Morley Knight 74
    Practising English rein handling 76

10. **Two-handed tandem driving** 77
    Twinning the reins 78
    The principles of two-handed driving 79
    Additional notes on two-rein handling 82
    The disadvantages of two-handed reins when compared with English reins 82

11. **One-handed tandem driving** 83
    Changing direction 83
    Holding the reins in one hand 83

Holding buckled reins in one hand 86
Notes on two famous tandem drivers 86

12. **Randem driving** 90
    The basic principles of randem driving 90
    Rein holding and turns 92
    Pitfalls to be avoided 93

13. **FEI Driving Trials: introduction and dressage** 94
    Modern international driving events 94
    Presentation 94
    Dressage: FEI Competition A 95
    The geometry of the figures 95
    The discipline of the gaits 95
    Tandem dressage tests 101
    The basic figures required in Dressage Test 3 (Advanced) 102
    Rules for tandem dressage competitions 108

14. **FEI Driving Trials: marathon** 109
    FEI Competition B 109
    Rules for tandems, Appendix M (1993) 109
    The marathon vehicle 109
    Safety measures in marathon tandem driving 112
    The rules of the course (1993) 112
    Sections A, B, C and D 113
    Section E – the obstacles zone 113
    Winter and spring tandem training 117
    Walking the course 119
    Fixed obstacles 121

15. FEI Driving Trials: obstacles 122
   FEI Competition C   122
   The principles of Competition C   123
   The circuit   124
   Training   124
   Competition driving   125
   A final word on marathon and obstacle
      driving   126

16. Tandem showing and other competitions   128
   The turnout of a tandem for showing   128
   British showing classes   131
   Different types of tandem   132
   Disabled drivers   135
   Other British tandem competitions   135

17. Tandem dressage, high school and higher equitation   136
   Dressage to music   136
   Tandem equitation   138
   Mounted tandems   138
   Equestrian tact and sensitivity of touch   140
   No foot, no horse!   141
   A last word   143

18. Final notes   144
   A two-day event in France   144
   In conclusion   146

   Bibliography   148
   Index   150

Acknowledgements

I should like to mention first the kind help of Catherine Drouin-Massu, a young Anglo-French lady, retired English teacher and lover of driving tandem with her horses and ponies. I also thank my editors Lesley Young who reshaped the text in her wonderful mother tongue which I am sure will be appreciated by the reader, and Elizabeth O'Beirne-Ranelagh, a very competent editor and benevolent, good-humoured young lady.

From Great Britain, I am very grateful to all those who trusted me, helped me and encouraged me to write *Driving a Tandem*: Sallie Walrond, Tom Coombs and many well-known members of the Tandem Club of Great Britain from England, Scotland and Wales.

I have also not forgotten Jack D. Pemberton of Canada and Barbara Weir of the USA.

From France, Paul and Sue de Brantes have been my main supporters, as well as Pierre de Chézelles, Président de l'association française d'attelage; Gabriel Fodor, vice-Président; Christian and Antoinette de Langlade; Maurice L. Perret, and André Grassart.

From Switzerland, I would like to thank Monsieur A. Dubey; Herbert Laesslé, President of the Swiss Tandem Club; J. J. Hänni; Heidi Keller and Karl Iseli. From Italy, I. Cinquini, in memoriam. From Belgium, Eric Andersen. From Holland, Tjeerd Velstra and Jan Maiburg, President of the Dutch Tandem Club. From Germany, Count Leopold and Lady Rothkirch; Michael Quinkler and Angelika Dreckman. From Sweden, Count H. Skiöldebrand.

Foreword

Dr Paul Doliveux is a skilled tandem driver in his own right, a dressage rider whose teacher was *Mestro* Nuno Oliveira and a distinguished orthopaedic surgeon who has made a close study of the physiology and psychology of horses. He has drawn extensively on all his knowledge and experience in writing a unique and very learned book about this esoteric form of coachmanship. In it he explains in erudite detail the various techniques which people have developed over the past 200 years for handling four reins to drive a tandem, as also a four-in-hand for which they are virtually identical, and he firmly favours and recommends the classic English method whose original conception he attributes to the English coachman Edwin Howlett.

There are some 30 regular tandem drivers in Britain and probably not more than about 300 in the whole world and Paul Doliveux's book will surely become their bible. It should also be of great interest to all horsemen, especially to all of those who drive their horses as well as ride them, being a profound study of the physical powers and limitations of horses and ponies, of their reactions to aids and stimuli and of comparisons between a number of different types and breeds, with particular reference to their suitability for work in harness.

The historical survey, which fills one chapter, and the numerous historical references and anecdotes interspersed throughout the text of the whole book, many of which appear in print for the first time, make fascinating reading and reflect the extent of Dr Doliveux's researches, as does the bibliography of 54 books in six different languages. The English text reveals that the author is not writing in his native language but he employs a most felicitous turn of phrase and his technical explanations are clarified by many well-drawn diagrams which complement the photographs and reproductions of fine paintings with which the book is profusely illustrated.

Paul Doliveux has combined a scholarly treatise with an instructional manual to produce an excellent book which must rank with the classics of the past and with Sallie Walrond's invaluable contemporary publications to deserve a prominent place on the shelves of all horse and harness enthusiasts.

Tom Coombs

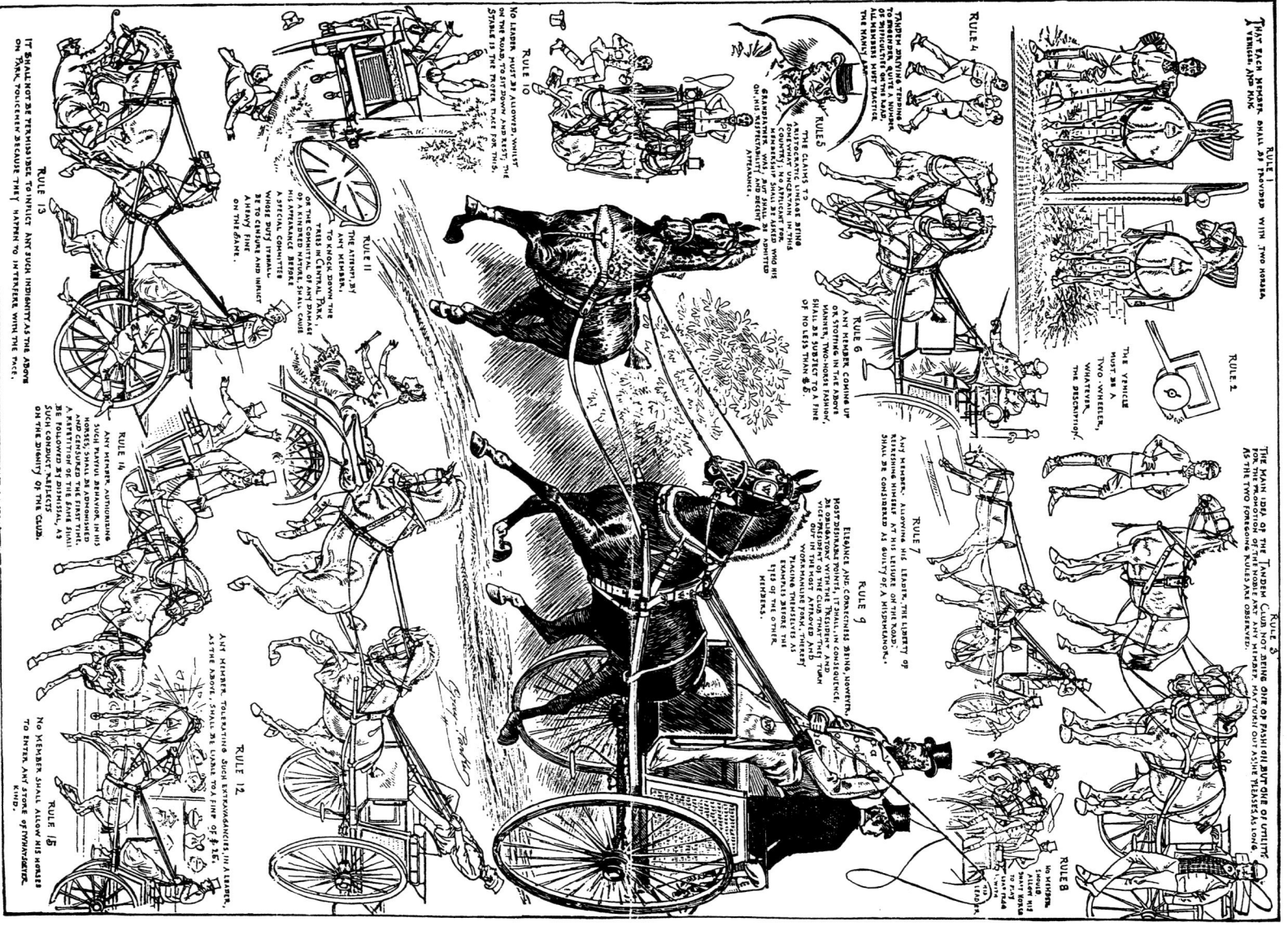

'Revised rules of the America Tandem Club'. (Gray-Parker 1900)

Introduction

Nearly a hundred years ago, at the beginning of the twentieth century, it was quite the done thing for four-in-hand and tandem drivers to give public demonstrations in cities such as Paris, in order to show off their skills in English rein handling. Such exhibitions of tandem driving were given by both ladies and gentlemen. Photographs exist showing a type of *concours de dressage* in the narrow Parisian streets, often involving turning an acute angle at the rue du Sabot. Along the avenues of the Bois de Boulogne, *concours d'obstacles* could be seen, twisting and turning between le Pavillon d'Armenonville and la Porte Maillot, where the drivers often stopped for a refreshing drink. European and American drivers of this period also crossed the Channel and the Atlantic to receive tuition from the great English master, Edwin Howlett.

The names of Arbuthnot, Duncan, Fairman-Rogers, Sandys, Tiffany and Winthorp are still remembered from those happy early days when many fashionable people came to Paris to learn to drive tandem and also to sample the excellence of French cooking and taste French wines.

'L' attelage en tandem'. (Toulouse-Lautrec 1897)

French tandem toy, nearly one hundred years old, driven by an English doll.

1
Traditional English tandem driving

What is a tandem?

In conventional equestrian terms, the word 'tandem' means a driving team of two light horses or ponies harnessed in single file to a two-wheeled carriage. The horse nearest the carriage is called the wheeler and the other is referred to as the leader.

Two heavy draught horses harnessed in single file to a tipcart or a piece of farming machinery cannot be called a tandem in the peerist's view, although the same team could be referred to as a tandem if it were put to a light carriage, as happens at National Haras (stud farm) shows in France.

Tandem driving through the years

For some time it was believed that tandem driving was invented by a certain English aristocrat called Lord Tandem, although there is no historical proof of the existence of this gentleman and no one really believes the story these days. Despite this, a few years ago, a young lady who is a good friend of mine and a very accomplished whip who drives a nice sporting tandem, was introduced by the announcer at a Saumur show as 'the great grand-daughter of Lord Tandem'. This came as a great surprise to my friend who was obviously the first young lady ever to drive a tandem in Saumur, but it does prove that the announcer had heard about the mythical lord.

In Latin, *tandem* means 'at length' and *Collins English Dictionary* gives driving two horses one behind the other as one definition of this word. The term was used to refer to carriage driving in the 1785 *Classical Dictionary of the Vulgar Tongue*, edited by E. Grose.

Tandem driving was already quite fashionable in the early 1800s. Among Cambridge University undergraduates of that time, tandem driving was considered to be an offence, as an edict of 1807 makes quite clear:

> We, the Vice-Chancellor and heads of the colleges, do hereby order and decree that if any person or persons *in status pupillari* shall be found driving any tandem and shall be duly convicted thereof before the Vice-Chancellor, such persons so offending shall, for the first offence, be suspended from taking his degree for one whole year, or be rusticated according to the circumstances of the case; and for the second offence be liable to such further punishment as it may happen to deserve, or be expelled from the University.

It would seem, therefore, that the first people to drive tandems were not regarded as very responsible. In the

Tandem of Shires, USA. (Achenbach *magazine, Switzerland*)

Duke of Beaufort's Badminton Library publication, *Driving* (1889), Major General Teesdale quotes a celebrated horse-dealer as saying: 'I always look upon a man who drives a tandem as a fool: he makes two horses do the work of one and most likely breaks his silly neck.'

In France, the oldest reference to the word 'tandem' is given in the *Grand Larousse Encyclopedic Dictionary*, which gives the source as 'Simon 1816'. In a study of English theatre of the same date, *Le Théâtre anglais de Londres*, the following description is given of a play entitled *Hit and*

'A swell turn out, 1804'. (Mario Broekhuis, El Arnhem, Holland)

Miss: 'One of the characters in the play "HIT & MISS" is a young lawyer who drives his tandem-cabriolet with two horses one in front of the other, which he overturns after running over an old woman, a form of behaviour which is not in accordance with our own customs but which, however, amused the spectators.'

It would seem from these references that tandem driving had already gained a somewhat dangerous reputation, although the President of the Netherlands Tandem Club recently gave me the following quotation: 'on April 14th 1814 the famous tandem ... which Mr Buxton backed himself to drive without letting his horses break their trot, from Hounslow to Hare Hatch, which is a distance of twenty-four miles, in two hours; which shows that careful driving was indeed possible and that tandem driving was already considered a sport by some skilful whips.

Despite this, tandem driving seems to have gone out of fashion to a certain extent by about 1840, for there are no important references to it in the interim.

The Crimean War (1853–6) provides the next reference of note to tandem driving. Very soon after the disembarkation of Anglo-French troops, battle ceased and the siege of Sebastopol began, which was to last for over a year. Queen Victoria's artillery officers did not get to fire their mounted guns very often and thus became extremely bored. In true British sporting tradition, they decided to organise a new, very rash and foolhardy race for tandem drivers by galloping two horses harnessed in tandem to a gun carriage. High speeds and high wagers were the order of the day! Once back at the Royal Academy in Woolwich, young officers relived their exploits by 'harnessing an ill assorted pair in line, pulling a two wheeled ordinary cart as solid as possible at vertiginous speed'.

A few years later, in 1860, the Tandem Club was formed, of which the rules were very simple. 'Club members abided by whichever rules they wished, the entrance fee to the Club was nil and annual subscription was under no circumstances to exceed the entrance fee.' Later, the club became more sophisticated, especially at the Hyde Park annual meet, where spectators were able to admire the most elegant tandems in England.

The establishment of the Tandem Club marked a revival in the popularity of tandem driving which, once again, must have made its presence felt in Cambridge for, on 22 February 1866, the Senate passed another edict on the subject, this time forbidding livery stable owners to hire out tandems to undergraduates.

To conclude the story of the birth of British tandem driving, although we know of its popularity and history, we still do not truly know why it was given the name of 'tandem', meaning 'at length'. However, imagine, if you will, that you have been transported back to the year 1860, to the Tandem Club at Woolwich, a club whose membership was made up of young officers who drove tandem teams for the love of sport, elegance, gambling and speed and to show their phlegmatic contempt for danger. Imagine them, weary of waiting for the arrival of an honourable member driving his tandem. Finally, a distinguished member quotes the opening lines of Cicero's first oration, *In Catalinam*: 'Quo usque tandem abutere Catalina patientia nostra!' ('How long, at length, Catalina, will you abuse our patience!'). Such humour obviously made a good impression at Woolwich and it soon became commonplace for members to shout each time a turnout took a long time to return: 'How long, at length, tandem, will this gentleman make us wait! Tandem, here he comes! Tandem, let us settle our accounts. You owe me £100!'

Such was the fashion at that time that English expressions travelled the world and soon drivers all over Europe were calling a sporting turnout of two horses harnessed in line 'a tandem', a name which has persisted to this day and is now accepted all over the world.

Accompanied by a totally inefficient groom, I regularly train my tandem on a neighbouring estate containing 200 hectares (490 acres) of woodland. On my return home, after two hours of anxious waiting, my wife welcomes me, in the typical dry humour that I love, with the greeting: 'Tandem! At length! Lunch is ready!'

2

My favourite horses and ponies for a tandem team

If you intend to harness a pair of horses side by side, it is essential to choose horses that are as well-matched as can be in respect of breed, sex, size, colour and markings, but, most of all, their paces must be as symmetrical as possible.

For a tandem, on the other hand, although very similar horses might have become the ideal in recent times, in the past much charm and elegance was to be found by cultivating the differences between the wheeler and the leader. Certainly, the horses of the Tandem Club of Woolwich were quite ill assorted!

In the days of modern competition, however, everything has changed, thanks to very thorough schooling, which is aimed at producing a wheeler and leader that can match their paces exactly in working, collected and extended trot. For this reason, it is important to choose horses that are, in many respects, as similar as a pair – same size, breeding, lightness and stamina – although the leader may be more elegant in action and also more intelligent, i.e. clever, intuitive, lively, animated and skilful.

When all is said and done, however, alongside the strength of the wheeler and the elegance of the leader, you must have 'presence'. You cannot hope to put together a good tandem with sluggish horses, while matching paces are absolutely essential.

I once used a wonderful stallion as a wheeler. He was very 'cold' in his mind but very 'hot' in his blood so that the only problem that occurred with him was if he happened to get too near to a mare in season. In the last twenty years I have used a succession of seven entires for ridden dressage and single driving and I must say that the one referred to above also made the best wheeler I have ever found for tandem driving.

It is not my aim here to review all possible breeds that are suitable for tandem driving. I shall consider only my own three favourite types: pure-bred trotters, Lusitanos and dressage horses and ponies.

English, American and French trotters

Racing trotters have a poor reputation as driving horses because once they have been fitted with American checkreins, which apply pressure through the upper bit, their paces become completely transformed in order to obtain

New York Trotting Club 1841. (William Youatt, The Horse, *G. W. Gorton, Philadelphia, 1845)*

the fantastic flying trot that is only suitable for race tracks. Reschooled trotters can make perfect horses for hunting and long-distance driving/riding, but retraining them for use in sports or dressage driving is impossible no matter how long is spent on their reschooling. The only trotter that can be used in driving competitions is a young horse that has not yet been raced and, certainly in France, such an animal is difficult to get hold of because every breeder believes that the horse he or she is selling might well be destined for a fabulous future and so nearly every youngster has had a test period of at least one year in an American upper bit.

It is much easier for us to go to Britain and purchase a descendant of the English Harness Trotter first bred in Norfolk.

Once, when I was strolling along the banks of the Seine in Paris, I paused at the showcase of a second-hand bookseller to browse through a book, *The Horse* by William Youatt, published in 1845, which contained a dissertation on the American Trotting Horse, itself descended from the famous Darley Arabian, and which also named various trotters that would be well known to turf enthusiasts. The practice of ruthless selection procedures and a very taxing training permitted the North Americans to make incredible progress in racing within only a few generations and it was not long before almost any owner who was able to prove that his horse could trot a mile in half a second less than his neighbour's horse could win fabulous prize money in competitions under rules adopted by the American Trotting Association of New York in 1841.

To add to the excitement, tandem races against the clock then made their appearance, although the actual term 'tandem' was not used because the word was not known at that time in New York. Instead, accounts of the time speak of 'a pair of horses one behind the other'. I was delighted to find that the book contained a picture of a racing tandem, together with a list of its remarkable performances: it had covered 73.4 km (45 miles) in 2 hours, 55 minutes and 30 seconds.

The print shows two horses of the same size (15 hh) harnessed to a hickory sulky weighing 50 kg (110 lb), wearing ultra-fine racing harness without American checkreins. The driver weighed 62 kg (137 lb) and drove two-handed. You will note that the two horses are trotting and that, behind the sulky, two other horses are being ridden in canter by supporters in order to incite the tandem horses and encourage the driver.

On the Centreville course in New York, even more fabulous tandems were to be seen, such as Mr Theal's tandem which trotted 161 km (100 miles) in ten hours at an average speed of 16 kph (10 mph) in 1834 to win a bet of $5,500!

Youatt also mentions the incredible longevity of these superstar tandem trotters, which were first broken to harness at the age of five or six at the latest but whose performances were still remarkable at the age of eighteen.

Lusitanos and high-school dressage horses

Some people do not believe that the conformation of a dressage horse can be adapted to the requirements of tandem driving competitions.

I am able to give a personal opinion on the Portuguese Lusitano because I was fortunate to enjoy the friendship of the world-famous rider, Master Nuno Oliveira. I well remember hearing him conduct lessons in Portuguese, Spanish, French or English and his distinctive manner of speech.

'What is to walk and what is to halt, Dr Doliveux?' he once asked me before going on to supply the answer himself:

When your King Louis XIII arrived at the cathedral of Notre Dame de Paris in a coach of great ceremony, before crossing the Seine he stopped where his horse was waiting for him, held by Pluvinel, his equerry, and he mounted his Lusitano, going to the front of the monumental door of entrance which was wide open for 'the king'. First of all, to prepare his horse to walk, he waited in a little 'piaffe', to collect him, and only then did he leave at the walk so that he, the king, entered on horseback the enormous gothic nave. Thus he continued walking up to the choir at the solemn tempo, resounding in the respectful silence of the mute great organs, to arrive at his place in the centre of the choir when he slowed the walk to a halt. There, on his Lusitano standing in strict immobility, he doffed his great felt hat to pray. That is to walk and to halt, Doctor!

So many times since I have recalled this lesson and even now, when my tandem leader is walking up the centre line of the dressage arena, from X, to halt exactly at G and remain solemnly immobile for ten long and carefully counted seconds, I say a prayer while waiting and preparing to perform rein-back.

I am well acquainted with the stud of the King of Portugal, who used to breed only black horses, in contrast to the King of Spain, who liked only pure white. The stud holds to the tradition of keeping stallions only for riding and mares only for driving and I have seen Senhor Athayde, manager of the stud, driving a good tandem turnout put to a perfectly varnished tandem cart. I witnessed this team perform true passage (from the Italian *spassegio*), showing a very collected trot with impressive elevation of the forelegs and a clearly marked moment of suspension. It is the interruption of the forward movement which turns passage into passage-on-the-spot, which is called piaffe.

With the introduction of tandem driving to music and as figures, style and paces become more free, I am sure

My Lusitano Nafal: half passage.

that one day we shall see the leader of a tandem team execute passage or piaffe in the dressage arena.

Nowadays many excellent dressage horses compete in tandem dressage. Indeed, a Swiss friend of mine, living in northern England, drives a tandem team of high quality Lipizzaners with great success.

Tandem of Lipizzaners driven by René Schoop, England.

Pony tandems

Grading standard for continental competitions

Grade A	10.2 hh or under
Grade B	10.2–12.2 hh
Grade C	12.2–13.2 hh
Grade D	13.2–14.2 hh

Grade A ponies are not as fashionable in France as in Britain but it must be said that Shetlands have proved their power and courage in coping with the obstacles of difficult tandem marathons.

Grades B and C usually compete together in national competitions.

Grade D ponies overcome the disadvantages of smaller ponies which have almost no lateral inflexion. They are also able to show something of the power and qualities of dressage horses, unlike smaller ponies.

In *Dressage et Manège*, published in 1897, Count de Comminges reports the opinion of Lady Georgiana of Kedleston, a keen tandem driver, 'She harnessed only ponies, though not preferring any particular English pony breed, and that means certainly in her mind that all of them are very good for tandem driving, but she said: "A desirable size for a pony is between 14 and 15 hh [i.e. Grade D] and the wheels of the carriage will have the correct height of 1.40 m [4.5 ft]."' That is what was called in my boyhood *un double-poney* and it is the type of pony I used to drive along the lanes of my grandmother's estate, which is why I am now so pleased to see pony tandem teams doing well in our modern competitions.

Still on the British side of the Channel, I noticed that, in

Lady Georgina Kedleston, 1908. ('Crafty')

1988–9, His Royal Highness Prince Philip had abandoned his four-in-hand team of Cleveland Bay horses from the royal stables in favour of black Fell Ponies. His Royal Highness is certainly a man who appreciates the qualities of good ponies for he rode polo ponies for many years.

Ponies make an excellent choice for tandem driving trials and long distance driving competitions because of their courageous temperament, their quick reactions and manoeuvrability and their endurance, which is due to some extent to their feet. In comparison with a horse, which has an enormous body and very long, slender limbs, ponies are very privileged. The horse has a very powerful heart which works to maintain a constant flow of blood throughout the body. The left side of the heart works as a forceful pump which, with the help of gravity, sends bright

Tandem of Welsh ponies. Biff Riley, Tandem Club meet, England 1990.

red, oxygenated blood to the feet. Unfortunately, however, the right part of the heart is comparatively weaker than the left because it acts as a suction pump, which is far less powerful than a force pump, and thus the upwards flow of dark blue, deoxygenated blood, returning to the heart, is much more difficult to achieve.

It is here that the foot of the horse comes to the aid of the heart through the use of an elastic plantar cushion which is situated directly beneath the coronet (vascular plexus) of each foot. With every step, each hoof acts as a small force pump, sending the blood upwards, and thus aiding the weak suction-pump action of the heart. Without

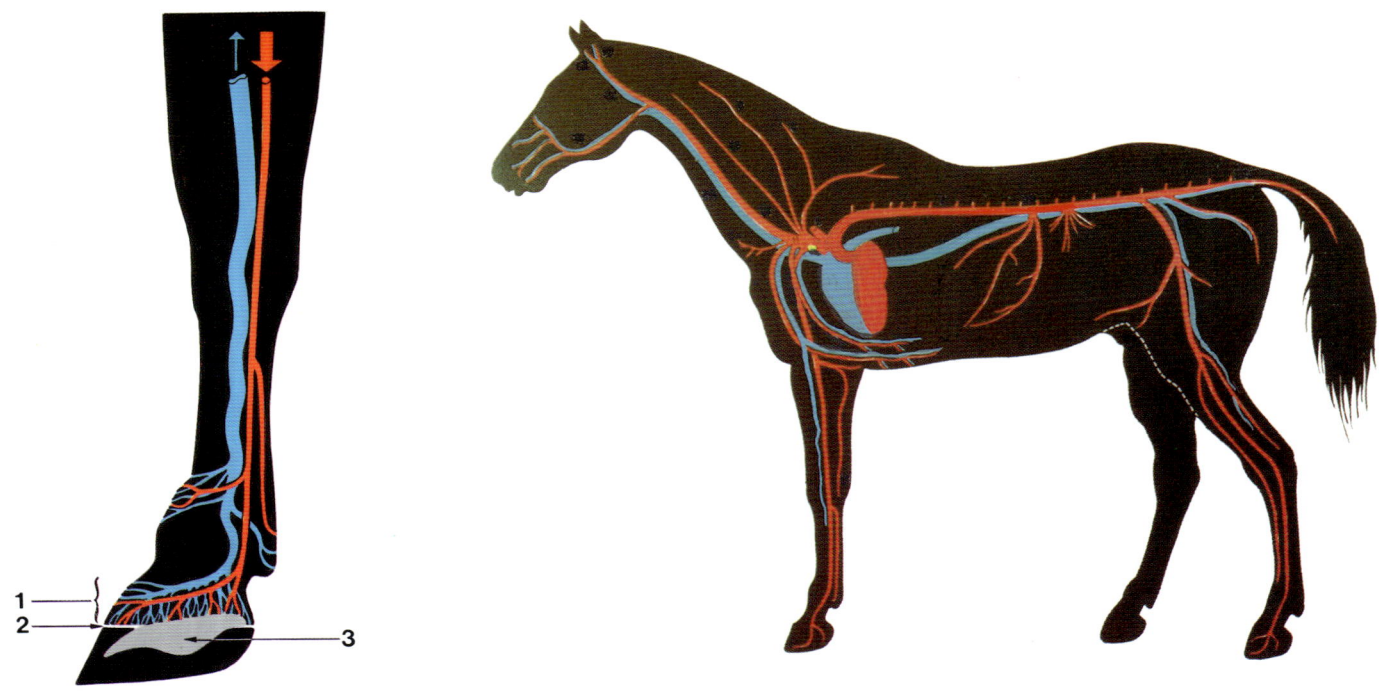

Circulatory systems of the foot. 1. Coronary plexus. 2. Coronet. 3. Elastic plantar cushion. (M. Berthélémy)

this well-organised system, horses could not gallop, trot or even walk. Without the blood supply provided by these four little peripheral pumps, horses would not be able to race without the circulation of blood failing, causing them to die of heart failure.

Ponies have exactly the same circulation system as the horse but their dynamic efficiency is superior due to their smaller size and mass, creating a shorter circuit but a larger and more active heart. Furthermore, a pony's feet are nearer to its heart, while the relatively quicker tempo of its trot also improves the return flow of venous blood to the heart.

Finally, the plantar cushion becomes smaller and smaller between ponies of Grades D and C and has nearly disappeared between Grades B and A. In consequence, when compared to the bigger horse, the pony is stronger, has more staying power and is less vulnerable in its foot.

Mark Broadbent, England 1980.

Choosing a pony

If you wish to buy a good pony, my advice is to go to Britain where you should find what you are looking for. However, be sure to choose exactly what you need and be careful when buying a young animal as, when a Grade D pony matures, it may become too big to compete as a pony and also be unsuitable for horse driving trials. Under international rules, both members of a tandem team must

Louis Droemond, Hamburg, 1992.

be either horses or ponies.

In France we mostly breed only British ponies, with the exception of a very nice Grade B–C from the Basque land of south-west France. The first pony I ever rode came from this area. This breed of pony is a Basque-Navarre into whose breeding Arab blood has been introduced.

Heavy ponies are very much a speciality of continental Europe, such as the Haflinger, which is mostly bred in the Tyrol, and the Norwegian Fjord. They are very fashionable for driving as a pair or four-in-hand and, as such, win many prizes, but they do not look so good as a tandem because they lack the desired conformation.

Ponies in tandem driving trials

Dressage Grade D ponies can do as well and sometimes better than horses in dressage tests because they usually bend well laterally. In the lower grades, the two ponies and their carriage remain almost in line on the geometrical curves of the dressage test, making the accuracy of the figures very much simpler to achieve. The judge tends to be uncomfortable with judging the paces if the ponies are too small.

Marathon and obstacle driving In marathon and obstacle driving the staying power, courage and aptitude of pony teams, together with the intelligence of the leader, commands the admiration of many a horse owner. Pony tandems negotiate obstacles easily, sometimes making quite incredible manoeuvres to save time. Their agility and stamina, enthusiasm, skill and cunning must all be taken into account. The polo pony estimates the position of the ball so that it can be won from an antagonist; the tandem pony estimates the ground and the obstacle gate so that a clean exit can be made at speed.

In conclusion, in chapter 6, on schooling a horse, especially for dressage, everything that I say should be read with equal interest by those who wish to drive a pony tandem, because the Grade D pony has a very promising and well-deserved future in tandem trials.

Other kinds of tandem – a tricycle. ('Crafty')

3

Tandem carts and carriages

In the British tradition, a tandem team is put to either a two-wheeled dog cart or a purpose-built, two-wheeled tandem cart. According to Sallie Walrond, a dog cart was:

> A general purpose vehicle which was found in most country coach houses and used for everyday occasions when a liveried coachman was not required. A Dog Cart was often used for taking luggage to the station, for shopping expeditions, for transporting the doctor on his rounds or the lawyer to his office. The two-wheeled variety [because there is also a four-wheeled type] was built for a single horse or a tandem. There was a seat for two people facing forward and another two facing the rear. The tail board lets down on two small chains to act as an adjustable foot board for the rear passengers ... Shooting dogs for the guns or greyhounds for coursing enthusiasts were carried under the seats [the box was too small to carry a pack of hounds for fox hunting]. The sides of the vehicle were slatted to provide ventilation. Some were hung on two side-springs, others on three or four springs. There was often some difficulty experienced in balancing the Dog Cart because if those in the rear seat were heavy, the vehicle was tipped backwards making travelling uncomfortable for everyone. Various ideas were tried to overcome this problem. One was to have sliding seats which could be adjusted as necessary. Another was the Level Balance, patented in 1883. The vehicle was constructed in such a way that by operating a lever the driver could move the body of the carriage backwards or forwards, on its under-carriage, to balance it as he required. Doyle's Patent Safety Rail was another invention thought of for the safety of rear-seat passengers. Some Dog Carts were

French tandem dogcart, property of Viscount Charles de la Rochefoucauld, 1910. (Achenbach *magazine, Switzerland*)

Tandem cocking cart. (Achenbach *magazine, Switzerland*)

built of mahogany and oak and were varnished. Others were highly painted. The shafts were usually straight and ran either outside or under the body.
(*The Encyclopaedia of Carriage Driving*)

Why, then, was the dog cart – a hunting carriage and dog transport – also the carriage used traditionally for driving a tandem? Crafty's simple answer is that the dog cart is:

'an outstanding vehicle in places where paths are still rudimentary and thus most often chosen by daring tandem owners' (*La Province à cheval*).

Because of its simplicity, solid build, rustic design and lightness in draught, the dog cart was also often used for purposes other than hunting. 'From these early Dog Carts were developed numerous types of Country Carts', called in France *charette Anglaises* (English carts). As the tandem was used for hunting, dog carts were usually the favoured vehicle, but tandem enthusiasts also often harnessed their two horses, one in front of the other, to whatever rustic carriage they owned, so that many varieties of two-wheeled carriage could be driven using a tandem team.

Carriage builders also marketed new models. An interesting new design was the Whitechapel cart, which was originally used by people working in the East End of London to take vegetables and fish to market. This cart was later redesigned and improved on by Henry Brewster, a famous London carriage manufacturer. It so happened that Brewster's brother James spent some time in New York, where an American tandem fanatic, Burton Mansfield, bought a Whitechapel cart in 1867. The Americans nicknamed Mansfield 'the father of the tandem' and when the Tandem Club of New York took up his carriage, it became a specialised tandem vehicle. (As a point of interest, the carriage-building business of the tandem brothers James and Henry Brewster was bought in 1925 by another famous partnership, Charles Stewart Rolls and Frederick Henry Royce!)

In the same way that any type of two-wheeled carriage could be harnessed to a tandem in England, so it was on the continent of Europe, where those few Frenchmen who did not wish to purchase a dog cart drove their tandem team put to a simple cabriolet, with one large seat for two people facing forward, as I myself have always done.

One reason why carriages were built exclusively for use in tandem driving is because of the great problem, experienced when using a dog cart, of the back-to-back position of the driver and groom, the latter being unable to watch the horses or the road ahead. Tandem drivers came to realise that they could dominate their horses more when seated higher up, and special tandem carriages were therefore built higher to accommodate this. The tandem carts still resembled dog carts but the carriage builders now incorporated an even higher forward-facing rear seat to enable the groom to supervise the horses over the head of the driver.

Tandem gigs had a single elevated seat, allowing the driver and groom to sit side by side. If the nineteenth century has been accused of delusions of grandeur, in the case of the tandem it soon became 'folly of heights'! Among gigs, the 'suicide gig' was certainly the highest of all. It was lampooned in a satirical drawing by Downing, showing two riders following close behind the team in order to be of help to the suicidal driver.

The cocking cart shown in an engraving by C. B. Newhouse also gives one pause for thought. The body was not very high but was surmounted by a box-seat resembling that of a coach. The body, slatted to provide ventilation, was too low to carry dogs but was ideal for fighting cocks. Cock fighting was frowned upon in some quarters, so gentlemen who were equally crazy about high-seat tandem driving and cock fighting were able to unite both passions when driving their cocks to the cock pit. Sallie Walrond recounts an anecdote about a well-known English tandem driver of the past who once took his bantam cocks to the pit in his cocking cart. Unfortunately, the cocks became travel sick, so there is now 'doubt regarding this explanation of the origin of the name. It could be that cocking carts were used as grandstands at cock fights rather than for the transportation of the birds.' It is also possible that the name comes from the strutting type of motion of that very high and curious tandem carriage, which might be thought to be reminiscent of the gait of a strutting cock.

To sum up, one can imagine a tandem team of horses or ponies being harnessed to the two-wheeled carriage of one's choice. In the British tradition, however, it was quite unheard of to use four-wheeled carts or carriages. A tandem cart with four wheels had simply never existed and for anyone to contemplate using such a vehicle to drive tandem would have been considered heresy by tandem purists of bygone days! Despite this, it was decided by the FEI in 1993 that if a driver so wished, he or she could choose a four-wheeled vehicle for modern tandem competitions at three-day events. The question remains, however – should such a turnout still be called a tandem?

These days, the range of elegant and traditional carriages at shows, dressage competitions and cone obstacle driving events is vast. Expensive and strictly accurate reproductions are produced by modern coach builders, following the designs of traditional tandem carts and gigs. So good are these copies that it is sometimes impossible to tell if the horses have been put between the shafts of an antique vehicle that has been carefully restored or of a completely new one, apart from the disc brakes and the iron wheels. Price does tend to become a vital consideration, which is why, fortunately, well-restored old tandem carts and pleasing gigs will always be with us.

It is still not absolutely necessary to drive tandem only with a carriage designed specifically for this mode of driving. Many types of gigs are very well suited to being driven in tandem using two well-presented horses in good harness. In FEI dressage tests, where five categories for general impression include one for presentation, two-wheeled carriages always score best in the opinion of the judges.

4

Tandem harness

Traditional English harness

For driving a British tandem put to a varnished country cart, which is a rather sporting turnout traditionally used for country driving, I very much like brown or tan leather harness. The light colour of the tan leather stands out well against the coat of a bay or dark brown horse or pony. Patent leather parts would be quite inappropriate here.

A more luxurious tandem equipage, such as two greys put to a dark-coloured Stanhope gig or something similar, should wear a harness with black patent leather parts and the fixtures should be made of brass or white metal.

In France, if the owner of the vehicle is a member of the old aristocracy, the harness will be decorated with the insignia of that particular, pre-Revolution, noble house; otherwise, the owner's initials or monogram must appear in the correct place.

Unfortunately, many old harnesses, which are usually engraved with the name of the harness maker on the back strap or on the saddle, become dangerous through the passage of time so that, eventually, the buckle straps (billets) will tear, requiring these parts to be renewed or repaired. When repairing old traces, it is possible to unstitch the existing traces, place a nylon trace between the two thicknesses of leather and then sew them together again. However, for safety's sake, it really is best to replace them entirely with new traces and billets.

Using additional harness furniture to create a 'ceremonial-style harness' is completely out of place for a tandem.

Harness for both horses

All measurements refer to medium-sized horse harness, suitable for, say, a 15 hh horse.

Bridles

Personally, I prefer hatchet-shaped blinkers, which may be covered in patent leather, as may the browband and the face-piece, whereas the cheekpieces, headpiece, throatlatch and noseband should be of plain leather. The ornamentation of the browband in dyed patent leather, metal or plastic is a matter of personal preference. A monogram may appear on the blinkers or sometimes on the rosettes but never on the face-piece.

Bits

So-called sporting bits are commonly used but I feel happiest with a pair of Buxtons dating from my mother's time, with a curved bar connecting the bottom ends of

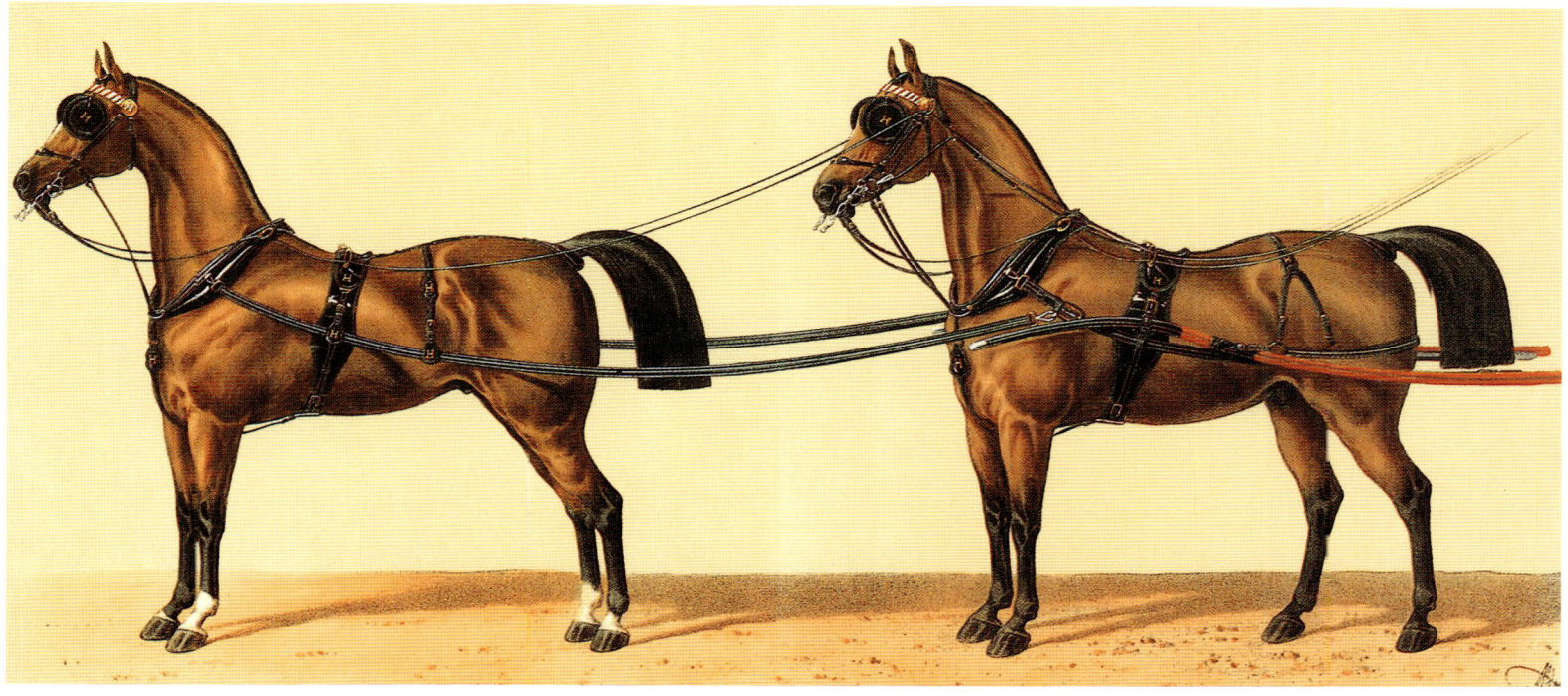

Typical English tandem harness. (Lené, Sellerie Française, *edited Brice Thomas, Paris 1920)*

the branches. My own two bits and their balanced curb chains are hand-forged and have leather or rubber bit shields, which are absolutely essential for all sliding-mouth bits. The bar connecting the bottom ends of the branches prevents the reins from becoming caught under the branches. I have always understood, perhaps wrongly, that *Liverpool bits* were traditionally more likely to be used for town turnouts and therefore should not be recommended for a tandem.

A pair of *elbow bits* should be easy to obtain and are quite in the British tradition, but they have no connecting bar and so are not suitable as the reins can get caught.

A pair of *snaffle bits* do not look quite so stylish or traditional but they are the best bitting arrangement for executing turns when driving well-trained horses or ponies.

Bearing reins, which were very fashionable about 1900,

are not seen so often these days because they cause so many faults and problems.

Collars

The two collars, which may be of different sizes depending on the build of the wheeler and leader, must be absolutely identical, including the hames, which are nowadays rarely covered with leather. My preference is for brown leather collars which are piped, light and well fitting. Patent leather is not traditional for collars, is too delicate for competition and ages badly. The hame tugs of the collars should have hame clips as there is a risk of an olive draught eye coming undone, particularly on the wheeler's collar.

The *false martingale* should be of plain leather. The leader may wear a patent leather drop bearing a monogram.

A *standing martingale* is strictly forbidden, but a false martingale looks good and is quite fashionable. Purists in my own immediate neighbourhood will accept brown, tan or yellow collars in combination with a black harness only for four-in-hand road coaches or drags, but old friends of mine, who originate from Belgium and who drive neither a coach nor a drag, always keep in their harness room tan collars combined with black harness for a pair. A little brown leather among all the black certainly brightens up the harness and no judge at any competition has ever reduced my marks because of my black tandem harness and tan collars.

Breast collars

Breast collars are tolerated, though not in the best tandem tradition. They are lighter in weight and do show off the horses' necks and conformation much better but are frequently adjusted too high or too low, so that sores often result. The best option is probably to choose a full collar for the wheeler and a breast collar for the leader. This latter collar must be equipped with a D-link, placed exactly in the centre, to which the false martingale may be fastened, so that the use of a left or right breast collar taken from a pair harness might be penalised by the judge.

The harness of the wheeler

Bridle

This must be provided with adjustable bridle terrets if the wheeler carries its head a little high. If properly adjusted, they then keep the leader's reins nearly horizontal. In fact, I much prefer terret rosettes or Roger rings with a roller bar to prevent the reins, or anything else, from getting caught up. Recently, large, oval Hungarian terrets, held down by a small strap, have become fashionable for marathons but they are certainly not suitable for a traditional tandem show.

Hame tugs

The hame tugs of the wheeler's collar must not exceed 40 cm ($15\frac{1}{2}$ in.) and must be of plain, supple, strong leather. A special steel buckle is used, which has a protrusion on the lower side, with an eye through which the spring cock-eye of the leader's trace is hooked.

The wheeler's saddle

This may be made of plain or patent leather and

must be wide enough and provided with two indispensable roller-bar terrets. The tug straps on the back band of the saddle must have holes to take the buckle tongue of the open tugs to allow easy adjustment of the balance of the two-wheeled carriage. There may be a monogram on the small top flap if it is made of patent leather. Sometimes the wheeler's saddle has no cantle, to prevent the reins from getting caught, and for this same reason a saddle with a flat top is better.

In France, a particular harness saddle is preferred to a pad as it simplifies the putting to of a two-wheeled carriage. Across the centre of this saddle runs a groove in which the back band lies. Before putting to, the independent back band, which is provided with open tugs, is attached to the shafts of the carriage which is then tipped backwards so that it rests on its supports. When the carriage is thus tipped backwards, the back band settles quite easily in the saddle groove and a safety strap then prevents it from slipping out again. This type of back band is very convenient when one has to put to alone but it does require the use of the special French saddle.

The wheeler's traces

Depending on the individual horse and carriage, the traces should measure between 1.6 and 1.7 m (5–$5\frac{1}{2}$ ft). They are adjusted at the front with the hame tug buckle of the collar or by the buckle of the breast collar.

For the rear attachments on the splinter bar of a dog cart, there are different types of fixing with appropriate safety devices.

The harness of the leader

Bridle

This should be simple, with rosettes bearing monograms as appropriate.

Saddle

This is finer and smaller than that of the wheeler, with smaller top flaps. A leather loop or keeper, through which the traces are passed, is sewn on to the flap at the correct height. This supports a trace on each side, which is the best method of preventing the traces from sliding up on to the leader's back if a serious mistake is made in rein handling.

There may be a monogram on the side of the saddle.

The leader's saddle may be replaced by a pad from a pair harness, but this is not really desirable in my view.

Trace bearer

This is attached to the back strap and must be placed well to the rear to be effective. It may carry a monogram on both sides. Trace bearers are not compulsory, however, and their absence will not be marked down at a show.

Leader traces or long traces

Their length depends on the type of tandem horses or ponies being driven. Nothing looks worse than to see the nose of the wheeler in the tail of the leader. On the other hand, too great a length becomes dangerous if a trace touches the ground when turning. The average length is 3.2 m ($10\frac{1}{2}$ ft), with five holes at the front, spaced 5 cm (2 in.) apart, for adjustment at the hame tug buckle or at the steel buckle of the breast collar. Rear attachment is provided by spring cock-eyes attached to the tug buckles of the wheeler's collar.

Tandem bars

These are not traditionally used in British tandem driving, although a few British drivers do use them. They are described fully on page 112.

Tandem reins (English reins)

The reins should be made of good quality leather. They should be strong and supple and of excellent make as rein handling is difficult enough under the best of circumstances. The leather should be tan-coloured so as not to dirty the gloves. Good grip is dependent on the width of the reins and therefore I would recommended about 24 mm (1 in.) for a man's hand and about 20 mm ($\frac{3}{4}$ in.) for a small woman's. The width of all four reins must be identical. It has been suggested elsewhere that narrower reins should be used for the leader but this seems rather stupid to me as the two narrower reins would slip too easily through the fingers.

A steel-tongued buckle is attached to the front of the reins, from which a strap called a rein billet extends for a maximum of 20 cm (8 in.). The purpose of this is to leave one hole for use in an emergency, for example, if the other hole should be accidentally torn by the tongue of the buckle.

For horses, the reins of the wheeler should measure 3.8 m ($12\frac{1}{2}$ ft) in length and those of the leader 6.4 m (21 ft). The reins should be made of long leather strips, neatly and correctly sewn together.

To reunite the wheeler's left and right reins at the ends, a small steel-tongued buckle is sewn on to the rein. The whip can unbuckle this with his or her right hand when desired.

If the reins are greasy, they will slip in the whip's hand, even when gloves are worn. The reins must be washed and soaped each week, hung up to dry overnight without any folds in them and then treated with glycerine saddle soap. Every two or three weeks, clean and dry the reins and then treat them with beeswax, which is good for the leather and prevents the reins from slipping through a gloved hand.

Traditional English harness and reins require regular maintenance each time they are used and should be stored during the winter in a cool, dry harness room, if possible inside a wooden chest or an old trunk, but never in polythene or plastic or in a room with central heating.

Accessories for a tandem equipage

In style, a tandem harness is rather sporting, therefore, in my opinion, a multiplicity of accessories is not desirable, i.e. I prefer no monograms, simple browbands, and the minimum of saddlery work.

Trace belly straps seem to me to be more dangerous than useful, although nowadays there is a fashionable type of trace belly strap which may be very convenient for obstacle driving.

Ear covers are a fashionable accessory on the continent of Europe and in international competitions, although they look rather like a 'bonnet' for draught horses or mules or the sort of thing a cab horse at the turn of the century

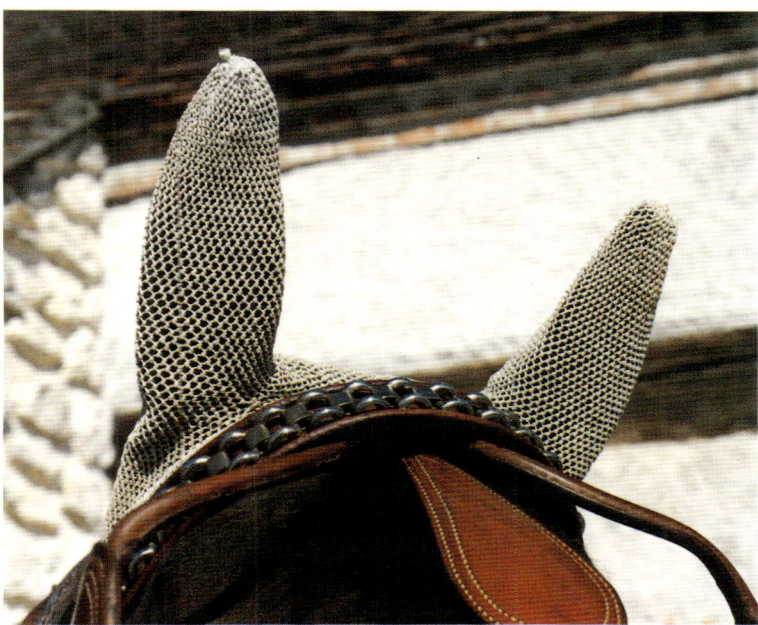

Net ear covers, made in 1920–30, France.

might have worn if waiting a long time before picking up a customer. This new trend is not so popular in Britain, especially not at the Tandem Club of Great Britain.

A few horses are particularly sensitive to flies, midges or other small biting insects, and people involved in horse racing sometimes make a horse wear an *ear net*, which covers only the ears. These nets are discreet, light and do not cause sweating. They can be found for sale at race courses or saddlers or ordered from a manufacturer and are much preferable to the ugly, tasteless, coloured bonnets, which I hope will disappear.

The traditional accessories of the nineteenth-century Woolwich Tandem Club are well worth preserving. British pragmatism is well recorded and thus, to avoid accidents, especially when driving a tandem turnout, whips were advised to make themselves known from a distance so that passers-by and other carriages would be alerted and could prepare to make way.

There were three main accessories: lamps, bell and horn.

For night driving, three tandem *lamps* were carried: a classic lamp on the left, another on the right and a third fixed in the centre of the dashboard. Thus, at night, if one saw a carriage with three lamps approaching, one knew to expect possible danger.

The *tandem bell* was quite large and deep in tone. It was attached to the throatlatch of the leader. A sterling silver bell was considered to be quite the thing at the club in Woolwich.

The *tandem horn* was placed in a special leather case attached to the left-hand side of the carriage. One might imagine that this horn was used to warn other people and drivers of the impending turn or the approach of this long equipage which had such a dangerous reputation among other carriage users in the streets of London and, indeed, that *was* its use by the occasional driver.

A *true* tandem driver or his groom, however, held quite a different opinion of the purpose of his musical instrument and viewed it as a serious competitor of the coach horn. The tandem horn was made of '36 Beaufort' brass and was between 70 cm (28 in.) and 81 cm (32 in.) in length. In shape, it was usually identical to a coach horn, being straight with a funnel-shaped end, although it was also sometimes rolled back at the end like a cornet or a bugle. In contrast, the coach horn was made of '44 Beaufort' copper and was 91.5 cm (36 in.) long.

The tandem horn could play the same notes as a coach horn but from a higher octave. These notes sounded 'start', 'clear the road', 'offside', 'nearside', 'pull up', 'steady', 'home' and the old English air 'Buy a broom'.

A tandem horn is even more difficult to play than a coach horn and everyone knows that the coach horn is impossible to play if one is not particularly gifted. I am reminded of the remark made by George Bernard Shaw: 'The main inconvenience of wind instruments is that they prolong the musician's life!'

My wife Claudie and I showing Ugueno and Phursac put to a French cabriolet with the hood open, Le Grand Chamoux, Brinay, 1992.

5

Putting to and moving off

Driving halters

When harnessing your horses, there is one rule that must be followed if you wish to avoid scratches on the blinkers. The bridle must be the last piece of harness that you put on before driving and the first piece that you take off afterwards. If you follow this rule, your leather blinkers will never be spoilt.

For this reason also, I always use very simple, light driving halters attached to a fairly long tether. These driving halters, which have no browband and only a double buckle down the right- or left-hand side, are quite easy to unfasten while the bridle remains on. Although a groom should be able to hold both tethers, he may, on occasion, happen to let go of one. For this reason, I ask my groom to hold only the leader after the wheeler has already been put to and its tether is fastened to a wall ring.

These light tethers can also be kept on underneath the bridles, with the tethers fastened correctly at the side of the neck. This is most convenient if you should happen to have to stop somewhere. Of course, a driving halter should never be worn during a show.

Putting the wheeler to a two-wheeled carriage in countries where one drives on the left

> The rules for putting a horse or horses into a vehicle are simple and should be strictly adhered to ...
>
> The [wheeler] stands harnessed with ... the reins looped through the offside terret on the saddle, in preparation for mounting.
>
> The vehicle is brought up from behind and the shafts are put through the tugs.
>
> The horse should never be backed into a private driving vehicle. This can result in a broken shaft tip, if he treads on it while the shafts are resting on the ground.
>
> The traces are hooked on to the trace hooks.
>
> The breeching straps are fastened round the shafts and traces going through the shaft staples ...
>
> If tandem bars are used, these are now hooked and buckled on to the hame chain ring on the shaft horse's collar and hame tug buckles.
>
> (Walrond, *Encyclopaedic of Carriage Driving*)

Putting the leader into position in countries where one drives on the left

> His reins are passed through the leading eye and saddle terrets on the shaft horse [wheeler]. Someone should stand to the left of the wheeler's head in order to hold both horses. The leader's reins can be taken in the left hand and the shaft horse's reins in the right hand. The lead traces are hooked on last, either to the bar or to the shaft horse's hame tug buckle.
>
> (Walrond, *Encyclopaedia of Carriage Driving*)

Moving off in my own country, where one drives on the right

I check one side, then check the other side, and am now ready to set off for a little drive along the roads of my neighbourhood, driving on the right. I shall mount on the left-hand side. The groom will stand on the right and should control both horses.

I check that my tandem whip is in place in the whip socket. This is always at the right-hand side, which is where the driver should sit whether he or she is French or British.

I stand on the wheeler's left side, the mounting side. I put my gloves on quietly and place my reins in the correct English hold in my left hand without taking up any contact with the bits. I speak in a very low voice and finally mount, telling my groom, still at the right-hand side, that I am *not* ready. I sit down on the right, wrapping my knee apron tidily round my hips, and take up my whip, which I unfurl to the right, holding the end of the thong. I always make a point of unfurling my whip before starting off in case it is needed.

Only then does the groom let go of the reins and come up to the head of the leader, while I slowly adjust my reins. As soon as I have a contact with the bits, we move off on voice command – the name of the horses being given in a low voice followed by a cheerful 'Come on!'

And so we start, *without* the groom. This is especially sensible if you are using young tandem horses and are worried that something untoward might happen. I do not like a speedy departure, so my groom goes on ahead, to the left of the leader and a good distance in front, and we leave quietly at walk. If all is going well, the groom gets into the moving carriage while the horses are walking along, which gives me sufficient time to furl my whip correctly after having just touched the hock of the leader if I feel he is not going forward enough.

When driving a nervous, lazy or new team, it may be necessary to move off quickly at trot because one of the most awkward things is to move off with horses that do not wish to go on or don't know how to move off properly because they are not sufficiently well educated.

On my return

One should always return slowly to the stables. I stop the team and then get down quickly on the right-hand side, while the groom jumps down on the left side to hold the leader. I take the horses out of the vehicle in the reverse order in which they were put to. Once back in their boxes and unharnessed, I give each a pat and a carrot before bidding them goodbye.

6
The schooling of tandem horses

In competition driving and in dressage, a well-driven tandem displays all the hard-won technical skill of the driver, coupled with the great elegance of the horses. The skill required of the driver makes this a sport which attracts only those who rejoice in the challenge of overcoming difficulties and who already have an excellent knowledge of horses and driving. It is certainly a challenge to drive a horse that is 6 m (20 ft) in front of you and almost free. I have only been able to succeed through the observance of two essential principles: a real communication with my horses and the use of refined schooling methods.

Terminology

At this point it is necessary to explain the terms that I shall use to refer to the position and movement of the horse's body and the driver's hands and fingers.
The three geometrical planes:
1. front (or anterior) and rear (or posterior)
2. left and right
3. upwards and downwards

The driver's fingers
In an English text it is difficult to give numbers to the fingers because they are numbered differently in English and French:
English: thumb, forefinger (1), middle finger (2), ring finger (3), little finger (4);
French: thumb (1), forefinger (2), middle finger (3), ring finger (4), little finger (5);
which leads English-speaking readers to believe that French people have five fingers and a thumb instead of four – a cause of great confusion when one is reading English and French texts on driving!

To pinch means to hold softly between the thumb and the fingertips.

To grip means to take a strong hold with the thumb and fingers and to use the palm of the hand as a support.

The driver's wrist
The grip on the reins can be supported by two special movements of the wrist.
1. Pronation is a movement of the closed fist, turning the back of the hand upwards.
2. Supination is a movement of the closed fist, turning the back of the hand downwards.

A dialogue between the driver and the tandem team

By 'dialogue', I mean the intimate and carefully 'worded' communication between the driver and each horse in the tandem.

The remarkable dialogue that takes place between a human being and a horse is unlike the normal conversation between two people because the horse has an extremely limited understanding of human words and, obviously, does not respond in words but communicates its moods and feelings by means of its bodily expression – sometimes happy, sometimes angry, sometimes co-operative. For this reason, I try to make talking to my horse a very simple matter by restricting the conversation so that we maintain a good level of understanding rather than a constant flow of chatter which is best kept for the loose box after work is over.

When training horses, the driver gives orders and the horse responds with a Pavlovian or conditioned reflex. Ivan Pavlov, a Russian scientist who won the Nobel prize in 1904, had made a study of the behaviour of a dog which showed its pleasure at the sight of a bowl of food by salivating. After several days of this, under identical circumstances and at exactly the same time, Pavlov gave the dog an empty bowl. Conditioned by the sight of the bowl at this time to expect food, the dog responded with high spirits and increased salivation. From this observation, Pavlov described the phenomenon of 'conditioned reflex' – an action induced by reflex and automatic response.

Following this principle, in order to converse with each horse of the tandem team, the driver will teach a Pavlovian reflex which will produce an automatic response from the horse. To create impulsion, the driver will give a stimulating call which will produce the conditioned reflex of forward movement in the horse. To restrain, the driver will give a steadying call which will produce the conditioned reflex of slowing down in the horse. In this way a dialogue is maintained between the human being, who commands, and the horse, who responds with a reflex action.

The voice of the driver

At this point, it is necessary to consider the make up of the human voice and also how it is heard by the horse. The human voice can produce a whole range of noises, from a clicking sound made with the tongue to a yell, groan, grunt, hum, whisper, whistle, hiss, etc.

The main characteristics of the voice are pitch (high or low inflexion), intensity (faint or loud) and resonance (the individual tone of each voice). By choosing the appropriate pitch, intensity and resonance, a wide range of commands becomes available to the driver. These commands can be adapted to suit the perceptive faculties of each horse in the tandem. Of course, to avoid confusing the horse, the vocal command must always be exactly the same for the same horse in the same circumstances.

How the horse hears the commands of the driver

In terms of pitch, both horses and humans register between twenty and twenty thousand vibrations per second, so there is no problem there. In respect of intensity, the horse is able to detect a yell as well as a whisper because its hearing is very acute. As for resonance, recognising the individual tone of its driver enables the horse to identify who it is that is giving commands.

The ability to determine where a noise comes from is well developed in the horse. You have only to watch a horse at liberty in a field to understand this. On hearing a strange sound, the horse will suddenly stop grazing and, at the same time, prick up its ears and look around to identify the source of the possible danger. When driven in tandem, of course, the horses cannot see their driver but, on hearing his or her voice, they can detect exactly who and where the driver is.

In this way we can see that the horse's ear transmits sounds to its brain where they are analysed and then an appropriate, often automatic, reaction results. The human voice is perfectly well recognised and analysed by the horse but the horse's brain does not think or reason, therefore a correct, quick and elaborate response will only be achieved if the commands are strictly limited. Conversation using whole grammatical sentences is not understood, so do not be talkative with your horse when driving.

The memory of the horse is excellent but limited, therefore the number of words used by the trainer must be reduced to a minimum, to include only interjections, simple words and the name of the horse.

Interjections are formed from the vowels *e*, *i* and *u* used with an ascending pitch, great intensity and lively resonance to provoke the reflex of impulsion, while the vowels *a* and *o* are used with a descending pitch, low intensity and grave resonance to produce a calming, slowing effect, as in 'Ho'.

Simple words are easily understood if used alone and about twenty should be enough. In the stable: over, steady, foot or lift; in work: forward, back up, right, left; in dressage: walk, trot, canter and halt.

However, the most vital simple keyword of all is the horse's own name. From the time of the ancient Egyptians and Assyrians to the present day, all domesticated horses have been taught to recognise their own name. To do this, simply call the horse's name on every occasion — when approaching it, patting, scolding, rewarding and above all when feeding. The earlier the name is taught, the better it will be memorised, although it is possible for a horse to learn to respond to a new name once or even twice in its lifetime. If each horse in the tandem team knows its name perfectly, you will be able to give selective commands to each individual by beginning the command with the horse's name. It is obviously vital for the driver to be able to address either or both horses with complete precision, beginning with the leader to control direction, followed by the wheeler to achieve pulling or backing.

Finally, other noises made by the voice are useful for addressing both horses together — clicking, gentle or shrill whistling, a hearty shout, etc.

To sum up, it is important to limit your language to the very simplest words and increase the intonation and pitch more than the intensity of the sound. Do not constantly repeat the same command once it has been obeyed, e.g. a continual 'trot, trot, trot' to a horse that is already trotting is a mistake. However, it is good practice always to repeat the same lesson in exactly the same way. Finally, take account of the circumstances you are in and of the horse's character and temperament and remember that 'The maximum is not the optimum' (Fechner-Weber Law). If you always shout very loudly, you will get a modest result and will also bore the horse!

Ten years ago I was invited to give my opinion on a

new tandem team of horses recently bought in Poland by a Frenchman who was very meticulous and pernickity about his way of driving. I was quite astonished to discover that he had a very strange way of talking to his horses and then I learned that he had actually taken the trouble to learn enough Polish to communicate with them more easily.

The circus tradition

Even today, the last great circuses of Europe continue to testify to the wonderful circus equestrian tradition. Among other marvellous presentations, one can see a mounted tandem, with the horse performing passage under saddle and the leader in Spanish trot, demonstrating the epitome of a tandem team that is fully familiar with simple and precise commands and a leader that is conditioned to respond to the voice and has respect for the whip. It is an unfortunate fact that the horse has a natural tendency to varying moods, including laziness and disobedience. If a circus horse does not instantly obey the voice of the trainer who is working on foot, the whip, or the threat of it alone, will teach the horse respect for the command given and you will never see circus dressage schooling being undertaken on foot without a whip in the hand of a trainer such as Alexis Gruss (France), Fredy Knie (Switzerland) or Christel Sembach-Krone (Germany).

The whip and the reflex response

I shall now describe the English whip, as used for driving tandem, with which I was first made familiar by *Driving Lessons*, written by Edwin Howlett while he was giving tandem and four-in-hand driving lessons in Paris in 1906. Tandem and four-in-hand whips do not differ in their three parts of stick, thong and lash, but the tandem stick is much lighter.

Dimensions The stick is 1.58 m (5 ft 2 in.) in length; the thong 3.72 m (12 ft 2 in.); the lash 20 cm (8 in.). These measurements are ideal for horses of 15 hh. The total length of whip and thong is 5.5 m (18 ft).

The stick is traditionally made of wood such as holly, but blackthorn makes the English whip *par excellence*. The wild blackthorn, *Prunus spinosa*, belonging to the rose family, is used all over Europe and not only provides splendid sticks but also a delicious liqueur! Craftsmen seeking perfection make solid, supple and elegant sticks, on which, 40 cm ($15\frac{1}{2}$ in.) from the upper end, they retain two small branches directed upwards in the form of a V. This greatly assists in catching the thong when furling as the little projections prevent the thong from unfurling itself spontaneously.

The stick handle is 20 cm (8 in.) long, bound by two silver or chromium-plated collars and covered in tanned pigskin.

The thong can be made from various materials such as white silk, cotton, whipcord or leather, either plaited or as a strip. The English thong is attached to the upper end of the stick by a fitting shaped like a swan's neck and made of whalebone or goose quill – the whole unit being called a bow-topped whip. Modern fittings are made of synthetic materials but are still fixed in the traditional way, by a slit graft bound in two strips of white leather and tied elegantly with black thread.

The lash, which is only necessary for those drivers who

wish to crack their whip, is made of whipcord or cotton.

Maintenance A good bow-topped whip must be hung up on a special, rounded piece of wood 10 cm (4 in.) in diameter, with a groove to catch the thong. The room in which it is kept should not be too dry – a cool tack room is best. After washing the thong, allow it to dry and then soap or oil the leather or use a special leather cream.

Nylon thongs are easily maintained but are also very stiff, most disagreeable to try to furl on the stick and will often unfurl spontaneously if not held in place with sticky tape. A good English whip is stylish, costly and easily damaged. If you are able to obtain a stick that separates into two parts, it is a good idea to keep it in a special tandem whip case. Your whip is a most important item of equipment but you will only really appreciate it as your knowledge and understanding of its use grow. I prefer a slightly heavy leather thong as a light thong is very awkward to catch and furl even when there is no breeze.

Handling the tandem whip

Let me say at once that handling an English whip from a tandem carriage seat in no way resembles the handling of a salmon fishing rod! A fly fisherman uses his wrist, whereas a good tandem driver uses mainly the arm and moves the wrist only a little. If you are able, I suggest that you film a first-class driver performing this movement as he or she strikes each horse in the team, and also the tricky procedure of furling. If you then run the film in slow motion, you will soon understand the art of the whip. None the less, the somewhat tediously complicated detail required to describe this procedure in written form is still indispensable in providing an accurate description of the technique.

Basic position

The driver sits up straight, with shoulders perpendicular to the carriage. The use of a seat cushion or box is indispensable for handling the whip with ease. Keep your feet flat on the floor or else on a foot rest inclined at an angle of around 30 degrees. The left foot should be in line with the carriage and the right foot slightly angled to the right, which will help to keep your shoulders permanently at right angles to the carriage. This is important if you are to keep a firm hold of the reins and will also help to make you look smart at a show.

The thong should be correctly furled on the stick – five or six turns only – and about 1.4 m (4 ft 6 in.) of thong should hang loose at the tip, forming a loop 70 cm ($27\frac{1}{2}$ in.) long. Following Howlett, I shall call this hanging loop the double thong.

Holding the whip

In accordance with show tradition, your closed hand must not cover the second silver ring but, if the balance of the whip requires it, you may place your fingers on this. The whip should be held out to the left at an angle of 30 degrees, with the forearm horizontal and the elbow close in to the body. The closed right hand should rest on the half-taut reins a little in front of the left hand. The lash or end of the leather thong should be held by the fingers. I prefer to hold the thong even more delicately, using the right middle finger alone.

Striking the wheeler

The double thong allows the driver to strike the horse sharply in front of the pad. This is achieved by a movement of the driver's arm, which requires the driver to bend forward slightly. The ability to strike the wheeler correctly is extremely important when the horse has to make a special effort in a difficult situation, often pulling the vehicle alone, and it would be a crime to use the bow top of an English whip to urge on the wheeler and risk breaking it.

Unfurling the whip and striking the leader

Sitting straight on the seat, I angle my whip at 45 degrees to my right, holding it horizontally to the right of the carriage. I then unfurl the thong by turning the stick between my fingers but still holding the lash under my middle finger. The unfurled thong then floats to the right in a large loop stretching from the tip of the whip to my middle finger, ready to strike to the right or to the left.

Striking the leader directly on its right

I carry my whip out to 90 degrees on my right-hand side, in line with my right arm and shoulder. I then release the thong which now hangs vertically and I immediately begin to describe a large circle: forwards, up to the left, backwards and down to the right. When the thong passes over my head, without the lash being allowed to make any sound, my whole arm is nearly vertical, and the movement is slow as the horses should not hear the whiz of the lash. Then I reach even further, continuing the circular movement to the right and as far forward as possible, aiming very quietly at the right hock of the leader. (Initially, when practising this manoeuvre, I would advise bending your body forwards and to the right.) I finish the movement with my weight on my right foot which is already slightly turned to the right. I then stop the movement without jerking or trying to bring my hand back and the lash strikes the leader neatly on the right thigh, hock or cannon bone and I 'feel' the correct stroke on the horse (or on an exercise stand in a practice session).

Striking the leader on the left side

This is done in almost the same way. I take the whip to the right, in line with my arm and shoulder, release the thong, which hangs down almost to the ground, and immediately begin to describe a large circle backwards with my whole arm, without bending the elbow – backwards, up to the left and forwards. When the thong passes over my head my arm is nearly vertical and the movement slow and soundless. I reach even further, continuing the circular movement to the left and as far as possible forwards and down, very quietly aiming approximately at the leader's left hock, which, as I am sitting to the right, I cannot see. (When practising this manoeuvre initially, I advise bending the body forward and to the left.) I finish the movement with my weight on my right foot which has been turned slightly to the left. I then stop my movement without jerking or trying to draw my hand back and the lash strikes the leader somewhere about the left hock and I feel the correct strike. Then I put my right foot back and slightly to the right.

Additional points

Leaning forwards is a technique for learners only as an

experienced tandem driver always uses the whip with a straight, motionless body and a dignified, upright head. You must aim low and must give the reins to the horses at the moment you strike them. Be aware of the hazards created by wind and trees etc.

Catching the thong
In my attempts to catch the thong in my right hand, I usually succeed three times out of four in bringing the thong directly back into my hand. If this fails, I then place my stick horizontally on my left forearm and fairly often the thong will land obligingly on this forearm beside the stick. I pull the stick to the right and take the thong in a gentle pinch hold between thumb and forefinger until the lash once again lies under the middle finger of my right hand. I then stretch out my right arm horizontally to the right, allowing a large loop of thong to hang on the right-hand side of the vehicle and stretching from the tip of the whip to my middle right finger. I am now ready to furl my whip.

Furling an English whip
It is not an easy matter to furl a whip using the right hand alone aided only by a thumb–forefinger pinch of the left hand which is also holding the reins. There are two different procedures.
1. Furling from right to left is described by Howlett in *Driving Lessons* as a large, horizontal, 180 degree movement of the stick, going from the right-hand side to the left, and manipulated in such a way that the thong furls clockwise round the stick.
2. Furling from left to right (Henri Baert) requires a more modest movement of the stick, through about 100 degrees, from the left-hand side to the right, backhand as it were, and manipulated in such a way that the thong furls anticlockwise. (See the illustrations on pp. 35–6.)

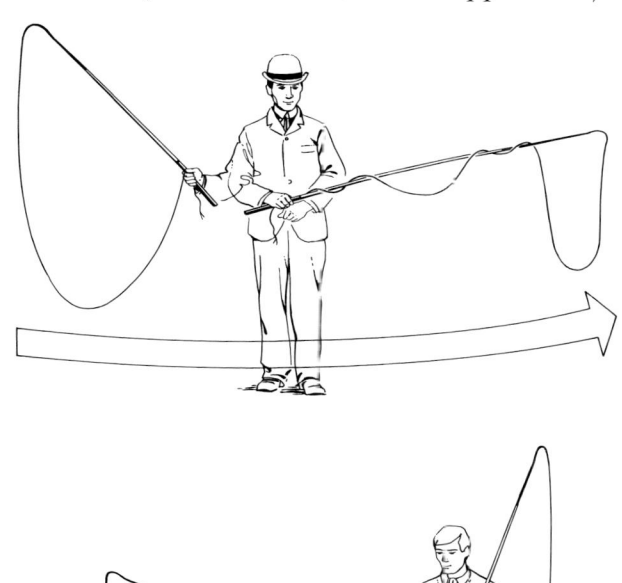

Furling the English whip. 1. Right to left (clockwise), after E. Howlett. 2. Left to right (anti-clockwise), after H. Baert. (Drawings by M. Berthélémy)

3. Practice in two steps of furling anti-clockwise.

Tandem whipping practice: drive.

Tandem whipping practice: backhand.

Final points on the use of the whip

You will need to practise using an English whip for months or even years to perfect the movements. I recommend exercises carried out sitting on the box seat of an old four-wheeled carriage with two stands placed in front of it to represent the horses.

When I go out with my tandem, I always begin with my English whip unfurled and call to my leader to set off. If the horse seems to hesitate, I touch his right or left hock gently with the thong at exactly the same moment as I call to him a second time. In this way I am sure to practise my English tandem whipping each time I go out.

My puzta whip

In order to furl more easily, I use my own special tandem whip for training and country driving. I acquired this from a Hungarian driver of my acquaintance who gave me the spare thong of his 'puzta' whip, which is composed of two parts. The upper part is a flat, supple leather lash 35 cm long by 1.5 cm wide ($13\frac{1}{2} \times \frac{1}{2}$ in. wide) which is firmly attached to the top of my 1.5 m (5 ft) ordinary French stick. The lower part is an ordinary leather thong 3 m (10 ft) long. The two parts are held together with a swivel and the whip furls and unfurls so easily that it is a pleasure to use and I carry it on nearly every tandem drive. I am so pleased with it that, at an annual meeting of the BDS Tandem Club, I presented our honourable President with a replica of my own new type of training whip, half-French, half-Hungarian, which I named my 'bastard whip', causing much merriment among those around me.

Furling my 'bastard' whip, so-called because it is half Hungarian and half French.

Conclusion

At the 1992 World Championship in Riesenbeck, some four-in-hand drivers carried a special bow-topped whip with a rotating bow (now patented in Germany). This new type of whip may one day completely revolutionise the available choice of tandem whips as it furls easily and looks no different to the traditional English tandem whip. Personally I do not like it.

7

Dressage schooling on the lunge

Driving a tandem correctly requires great subtlety and therefore the schooling of the horses must be done to a high standard.

The thorough and meticulous preparation of the horses is essential for any driver who wishes to participate at a tandem show or in the increasingly popular tandem dressage competitions, especially tandem dressage to music. The dressage test demands fairly difficult figures from a tandem team and it is only possible to obtain the three good trotting paces, to rein back harmoniously, and to bend the horses correctly on a circle or through a corner if they have been perfectly and thoroughly schooled.

Whether driving for pleasure or taking part in distance or sporting competition driving, the tandem driver will soon become discouraged by the constant problems posed by trying to keep badly trained horses in line and will become even more disheartened if an accident should occur. If such a driver has chosen horses with a fiery temperament in the hope of producing the impulsion he or she has been unable to instil in them through schooling, disaster will constantly threaten.

For ease of handling, pleasure and safety to prevail, tandem horses must be well trained. It then becomes a great joy to drive a light-mouthed team at a brisk trot through the countryside.

The dressage schooling methods I use to train my driving horses are the culmination of twenty years' experience of ridden dressage in the past. It was during this time that I acquired the wide variety of knowledge that I now put into practice in driving and which has proved useful and effective. In this respect I am also grateful for the teaching of the old masters of equitation of Portugal, Germany and Vienna during the eighteenth and nineteenth centuries, especially that of Gustav Steinbrecht, riding master of that time at the Seegerhof in Berlin, who published a wonderful book entitled *Gymnasium des Pferdes*. This was a most apt title because in German-speaking countries a gymnasium is not only a school but an academy of advanced learning. However, the word gymnasium has quite different connotations in English and therefore I have decided to use the term 'schooling' in the following chapters.

NB: Please note that in the following sections certain assumptions will be made.

1. Dimensions of circles are given as a diameter only.
2. I shall always give the example of a horse circling to the left.
3. Illustrations will also only show horses travelling, turning or bending to the left.

Lungeing equipment. The side reins are adjusted for a bend to the left. The right side rein is taut and supports the right shoulder and the right hindquarter.

Lungeing equipment

1. A lunge rein which must not be much longer than the width of the schooling area.
2. A snaffle bridle without blinkers.
3. A snaffle bit. The 'long-cheeked snaffle' used in Vienna, also called a 'needle-bit' in France, or a Fulmer, is the most stable bit in the horse's mouth, due to the action of two leather keepers which prevent the bit from moving.
4. A classic leather lungeing cavesson, reinforced with steel, is worn over the bridle and fitted above or beneath the bit depending on the temperament of the horse. The

cavesson must rest on the bone of the nose, not on the cartilage lower down, where it would interfere with the horse's breathing. The noseband must be fitted tightly so that the cavesson cannot slip round to the side and injure the horse's eye.

5. A good quality, leather dressage roller, equipped with six buckles on the forward edge at each side, to which side reins can be attached. A pad is recommended.

6. Two side reins (110 cm/43 in. long for a 15 hh horse) with a swivel at the end of each. Along the last 40 cm ($15\frac{1}{2}$ in.) of the free end of each side rein about fifteen holes are punched in order to attach the reins to the buckles on the roller and to adjust the tension.

7. The girth should be adjustable at both sides because it is essential for the roller's stability that it is buckled very tightly and then retightened after a few minutes' work.

8. Three whips are necessary. My ordinary tandem whip, which has a swivel, is handier than the customary lunge whip when working with a long lunge line; a classic or ordinary lungeing whip is used when working with a half-length lunge line; and a dressage whip is used near the horse when working on a short lunge line.

The benefits of lungeing the tandem horse

An animal will make a good tandem horse if it learns what it is being asked to do through the communication that can be established during lungeing, i.e.:
- If it is active, thanks to the impulsion produced and maintained by the reflex conditioning created by the whip while the horse is working on the lunge.
- If it knows how to bend, thanks to training on the lunge on circles and through corners. In tandem driving, of course, the wheeler, who is held between the shafts, is only able to bend its neck, but the leader is able to bend its neck and also through its spine.
- If it has been able to work in a good indoor riding school or outdoor manège with well-drained, sandy footing. I work in a 16 × 40 m ($17\frac{1}{2}$ × $43\frac{1}{2}$ yd) arena and have the benefit of a very convenient stone wall along one long side. The corners of the schooling area must be clearly marked using two long white bars set at 90 degrees, as the lateral flexion of the horse in the corners is most important in schooling. Lungeing in an open field or along a fence is not adequate.

Depending on the length of lunge line to be used, three objectives may be achieved:
- The long lunge line helps to produce impulsion.
- The half-lunge line helps to produce impulsion and flexion.
- The short lunge line helps to produce impulsion, flexion and collection.

NB: Please note that it is essential for the trainer to wear a sturdy pair of gloves!

Work on the long lunge line

The lunge line must be held in the following manner.
1. Whether the horse goes round to the left or to the right, the lunge line is always held in the left hand. The line must be looped correctly. The right hand holds the whip and also helps in shortening or lengthening the lunge line by using a pinching movement of the thumb and forefinger.

Holding the half-length lunge line as in an English four-rein hold, which helps to practise the rein hold.

2. I hold the lunge line in the same way as I hold my English tandem driving reins, i.e. in a left-hand grip, no matter which direction the horse is circling in. As you will see in the illustration, I make loops with the help of my right hand.
• The first loop is held between thumb and forefinger and represents the left lead rein.
• The second loop passes between the left forefinger and the middle finger and represents the right lead rein which would lie on top of the left wheel rein.
• The third loop passes between my left middle finger and ring finger and represents the right wheel rein.

In this way, using the lunge line, I simulate exactly the left-handed manner of holding a set of tandem driving reins. Adopting this practice helps to teach the correct way of holding the reins and also increases the strength and staying power of the fingers of my left hand, particularly the ring and little fingers, which are always weaker than the other fingers. Holding the lunge line in my left hand in this way, just like a set of English reins, is possibly unique to my own training methods but really is an opportune way of exercising and strengthening my old left fingers.

3. The tandem training whip should be held between the right thumb and forefinger, with which you will also be able to take in or let out additional loops of the lunge line and coil them in sequence over the left hand.

4. It is now possible to practise using my right fingers just as I would in English rein handling. I can adjust the tension of the lunge with my right hand, as I would the rein when the horse is turning, and I can work on improving the strength and skill of three different finger holds.

(i) The right forefinger alone can be used to grip the lunge line as it would the left lead rein. Having three flexor tendons instead of two, as all the other fingers have, this finger is very strong.

(ii) The right middle finger alone can be used in exactly the same way as it would on the left wheel rein as this finger is also strong, although less independent than the forefinger.

(iii) The grip of the ring finger combined with the little finger works just as it would on the right lead and right wheel reins jointly. These two fingers are quite weak in comparison with the other fingers and much less independent. In driving, however, they are required to

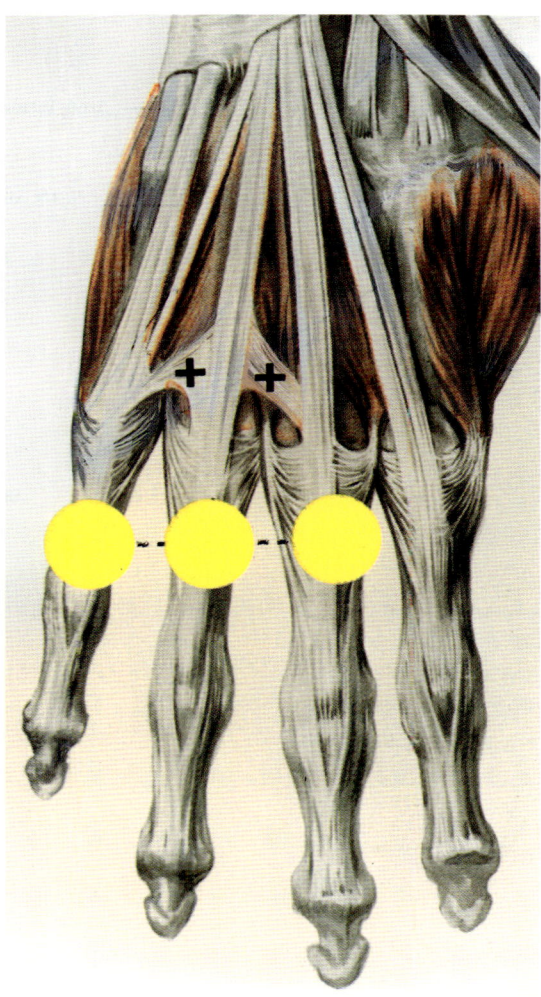

Back of the right hand. The ring finger is connected by small ligaments (+ +) to the middle finger and the little finger. (M. Berthélémy)

control two reins together, so exercising and strengthening them through such practice is very important. When these fingers grip, the extensor tendons in the back of the hand slacken, otherwise flexion would prove impossible, but the flexion is weak, which explains why these two fingers lack strength and become stiff or cramp up easily when used singly and why such training is good for them (see illustration). Music lovers will perhaps recall how Robert Schumann sought to acquire the skill that the great violinist Paganini had in his fingers by playing scales on the piano with his forefinger and middle finger tied together, thus exercising and training his ring and little fingers alone.

Handling the tandem whip

I must stress again that I always hold my lunge line correctly looped in my left hand and that my right hand is always responsible for the whip, regardless of the direction in which the horse is circling – exactly like a tandem driver sitting on the box seat.

1. When the horse circles to the left, I start my right stroke with a large circle – forwards, to the left, backwards and to the right – and then, having completed the circle, I continue forwards in the direction of the horse's near hind foot. I finish this right swing with my right knee slightly bent and my weight on my right leg.

2. When the horse circles to the right, I start a backhand strike and continue with a large circle backwards, to the right and forwards, aiming at the off hind foot. I finish the backswing with my right knee bent and my weight on my right leg with my right foot turned slightly to the left.

3. Consequently, during lungeing sessions, you can practise with the lunge line and the whip at the same time.

Practice with the whip on the long lunge: (top) start; (centre) drive; (bottom) backhand.

A working session on the long lunge

Throughout all the work in which the horse retains its comparative freedom, it is most important to maintain the special dialogue between horse and trainer that is created by the compromise between the voice that commands and the whip that threatens or even touches the hock. It is while working on the lunge that this dialogue is taught, which will allow impulsion to be activated and maintained.

1. Relaxing the horse without side reins

Allow the horse to go round without side reins at first, both to the left and to the right, at whatever pace it wishes, to work off any freshness.

2. Attaching the side reins

After relaxation, I attach the side reins to be very, very long as there will always be time to shorten them progressively later on and, anyway, I never check any exuberance with a brutal pull on the cavesson. To obtain an active trot and send the horse forward sufficiently to keep the lunge taut, the horse needs to slow down progressively. If the horse is very nervous, I use a trot–canter–trot dialogue for as long as is necessary.

3. Work in trot on large circles

I begin my lesson by using first voice then whip. By noting the success of this, I can then adjust the pitch, resonance and greater or lesser intensity of my voice.

I decrease the circle from 15 m (49 ft) diameter to about 6 m (20 ft), at which distance I can touch the hock with the thong of my whip, and then increase it again to 15 m. The horse quickly understands that, at about 6 m, it is in a 'danger' zone and this is the zone in which it is most convenient to work with the voice and the threat of the whip only, by raising the stick for a few seconds immediately after the spoken command and then instantly lowering it to the ground again. If the pressure lessens and the lunge rein slackens, however, you must again resume the use of voice and then whip thong touching the hock. Increase the circle to 15 m (49 ft), let the horse go on quietly and then decrease the circle to 6 m (20 ft) again.

The practice of working the horse on a straight line along the wall between the execution of two circles is excellent for creating impulsion. When the horse arrives at the wall, you must slacken the lunge line, use your voice, threaten with the whip and run a few steps parallel to the wall. When asking for the return on to a circle in a good cadence, the lunge line tightens and the horse follows the circle, bending its neck slightly. This exercise teaches impulsion on a straight line and on large circles.

4. Procedure
- Begin a circle to the left.
- Use voice, then whip thong touching the hock gently. Increase the circle. Decrease the circle.
- Use voice without whip. The horse must go forward energetically under the influence of conditioned reflex, without the use of the whip. Increase the circle. Decrease the circle. Decrease again. Continue decreasing the circle until the horse stops near you.
- Halt. Reward. Pat. Change sides to the right, quietly shortening the lunge line in nice long loops, neatly coiled and always in your left hand.
- When working the circle to the right, your right hand will carry and move the whip in a backhand motion. Follow the same programme as outlined above.

It is worth making the effort to learn how to crack a whip when training horses for a tandem team but it is important to reserve the element of surprise inherent in the sound specifically for the leader. For this reason, I crack my whip constantly while schooling the wheeler on the lunge, so that this horse becomes progressively bored by it, while the leader, who is not so accustomed to hearing the crack of the whip, will always rush forward immediately. In this way I can practise cracking the whip in both straight strokes and backhand but only when lungeing the wheeler.

Conclusion
Work on a long lunge line allows the trainer to study the horse as it goes round, just as an orthopaedic medical student learns to study the walk of his or her patients. You must note the physical performance of the horse from the hindquarters to the forehand.

When the horse trots, its physical behaviour changes continually in three dimensions:
(i) in its length – study the engagement of the haunches;
(ii) in its width – look for correct lateral flexion of the back and neck following the curve;
(iii) in its height – study the position of the neck, poll and nose.

You must also analyse the psychological reaction of the horse in terms of the dialogue you wish to establish and continue to activate, just as a speaker does to prevent an audience from falling asleep or when a teacher encourages a child in order to guard against encroaching laziness. This observation of the horse becomes even more important when it works on the half-length lunge line.

Work on the half-length lunge

Bending is a fundamental requirement of refined or advanced schooling.
- When a horse is working on a bend, it must not carry its outer hind leg out of the circle and you must make sure that it engages its inner hind leg under its body on the inner side of the circle, thus encouraging it to collect. A horse that is being lunged on a 15 m (49 ft) circle does not bend naturally – and on a larger circle even less so. However, when a horse is being lunged on circles of between 10 and 6 m (33–20 ft), using a half-length lunge line, it must bend in order to follow the curve of the circle.
- Unlike the long lunge line, the half-length lunge line is held in the left hand when circling to the left and in the right hand when circling to the right, thus necessitating the changeover of the whip from one hand to the other.

Flexion and bending

Flexion When the horse goes round to the left on the half-length lunge, it follows the turn with its eyes and must therefore bend its neck slightly in the direction of the turn. This is called the flexion of the neck. Such flexion involves bending one side or the other of the cervical vertebrae in the horse's neck. In other words, here flexion means lateral flexion or sideways flexion.

Bend The outline of a horse on a circle is only correct if the track of the hind legs follows exactly in the track of the forelegs. In order for this to happen, it is necessary for the horse to bend along the whole length of its spine – through the cervical vertebrae of the neck and dorsal and lumbar vertebrae of the back.

The bending of the whole spine is also referred to as lateral bending and I shall use this term as well as side bending.

When teaching the horse to bend

If the horse's hind legs are carried to the outside or inside of the circle, the horse is said to be resisting the bend and this is a major fault.

Lateral flexion will become more pronounced when the horse is worked on a smaller circle, therefore it is necessary to decrease the size of the circle gradually, making the lunge line progressively shorter. The risk of the quarters swinging out increases if the circle is reduced too much – on the half-length lunge line it should never be less than 6 m (20 ft) in diameter.

A good way to prevent the quarters from swinging out is to work the horse on a 6-m circle in a corner as then the physical limitations of the corner will hold the hind quarters in on half the circle.

Side reins

The use of side reins can limit the swinging out of the hind legs on a 6 m circle. (At this point I will remind the reader that a corner in an official tandem dressage test represents a quarter of a 10-m (33 ft) diameter circle.)

When the horse goes round to the left, the lunge rein has a directing effect which pulls the forehand to the left and, in theory, keeps the forelegs on the circle, so that the neck will bend to the left. The lateral flexion of the neck to the left produces the following effect on the side reins: it slackens the left inner side rein and tightens the right outer side rein, which prevents the horse from falling in through its left shoulder.

Throughout this, however, the outer side rein is also taut against the convex bend of the entire outline so that it supports the outside hind leg and prevents it from swinging out. Adjusting the side reins to be too short is counter-productive because this increases the danger of producing the wrong flexion, cramping of the outline and an exaggerated swinging out of the croup. For this reason, it is better to allow the side reins to be too long rather than too short.

The support of the outer hind leg by means of the outer side rein simulates the support given by the right driving rein in turning left. This has the effect of preventing the croup from swinging out and, consequently, helps to engage the inner hind leg underneath the body. It must always be remembered that good engagement of the hind legs underneath the body is the beginning of collection.

The tension of the outer side rein on the lunge and the tension of the two outer reins held by the tandem driver have the same effect, namely in supporting the shoulder and the croup of the two horses in line, which results in keeping them on the circle and in the collection of the team.

Equipment
The long lunge line is looped in the ordinary way and coiled progressively to achieve the radius of a 6-m (20 ft) circle. It is always held in the left hand.

In contrast, the half-length lunge line is gripped in the fingers of the entire hand and transferred to the other hand when there is a change of direction.

When working on the half-length lunge, I give up my tandem whip in favour of a dressage whip 1.6 m (3 ft 3 in.) long, extended by a leather thong of 60 cm (2 ft) in length.

Obviously, it will now be necessary to change the whip over from one hand to the other.

Work on circles on the half-length lunge
- Your aim is to teach and perfect lateral flexion, without allowing the croup to swing out, and to encourage the engagement of the inner hind leg under the body.
- On circles, begin with a circle that is 10 m (33 ft) in diameter and progressively decrease this to no less than 6 m (20 ft).
- *Discipline:* working trot on the 6 m circle should be energetic and rhythmical, thanks to the whip, which creates impulsion, while the lunge line creates lateral flexion.

The use of the whip
Holding the whip in your right hand will activate the horse when circling to the left.

As the horse approaches the corner on a 10-m circle to the left, I keep my right hand low and the end of the thong of the dressage whip just above the ground, pointing towards the inner hind foot.

To activate the horse on the circle, I move my whip from the direction of the inner left hind leg as far as the direction of the left shoulder, making the thong whistle gently but

Six-metre diameter circle on the half-length lunge.

1. Slacken lunge line in the corner.

2. Half-halt (light tension, open thumb).

3. Halt (strong tension, strong grip).

without touching the horse. This action is preceded by a quiet, low, vocal command which is best explained by the German verb *treiben*, which is usually translated as 'drive' but has also the meaning of 'push, incite, press, excite, chase'! At this point, the reader must excuse my use of translations of four German commands which are used to restrain the horse. At the same time as these vocal commands are given, the left hand checks the horse by means of one of four different uses of either tension or a jerk on the lunge line.

Traditional commands used in German-speaking countries
- 'Half-halt!' – accompanied by permanent and light tension on the lunge line;
- 'Halt!' – accompanied by permanent and strong tension on the lunge line;
- 'Half-stop!' – accompanied by a supple jerk on the lunge line;
- 'Dead stop!' – accompanied by very strong and repeated jerks on the lunge line.

Method
(See illustrations.)

The half-halt consists of an isolated contraction of the ring and little fingers on the lunge, using a still hand that is raised slightly, with the forefinger open. This is the gentlest aid a lunge line can communicate to a horse that has already received some schooling.

The halt consists of the simultaneous contraction of all five fingers to produce a total grip with the left fist immobile and rigid on the taut lunge line but the hand raised higher.

The supple half-stop consists of an upwards tug with the left hand. The lunge line must not be pulled horizontally but must be lifted.

The dead stop consists of sharp jerks on the cavesson to bring the horse to order and to correct the disobedience of rushing. The very sharp effect of this action will produce an immediate stop. It is a manoeuvre that should only be used in exceptional circumstances but may need to be repeated two or three times in order to gain control of over-excited young horses and is something that the trainer must undertake with courage.

The use of the hands

By alternating the actions of the hand holding the whip and the hand holding the lunge line, you should achieve a finely balanced compromise of three factors:

(i) Impulsion, created by the whip.
(ii) Collection, achieved through alternating half-halts and 'vibrating' halts.
(iii) Relaxation, which will liberate the impulsion.

It is the quality of this compromise that will dictate the quality of the horse's lateral flexion on a circle in the corner, with the horse showing impulsion plus collection plus suppleness. A horse that does not work correctly loses its rhythm, carries its hind quarters outside the circle by falling in through its inner shoulder and becomes stiffer and stiffer until it begins to develop cramp.

Muscular contraction and cramping
Contraction is the normal physiological action of the muscles, producing a supple movement. For example, a person walks by flexing and then extending the leg muscles. The horse walks in a similar way.

Cramping is a prolonged, involuntary contraction of the muscles to produce stiffness. It will then block parts of the movement so that the horse cannot bend through the corner. The psychological make up of the horse, inherited from its nomadic ancestors, creates an anxiety about being trapped in the corner, so that it hesitates on going in and quickens when coming out of it. You must make sure that the horse submits to the exercise willingly and is not forced. The energy produced should be relaxed energy.

After several 10-m (33 ft) circles in the corner, to accustom the horse to the exercise, you can then discreetly show the horse the whip, after first using your voice, to maintain impulsion without cramping. Only then should the diameter of the circle be progressively reduced to 6 m ($19\frac{1}{2}$ ft) until the moment when the horse goes into the corner without hesitation and without cramping.

Working on a 6-m circle in the corner
In this way, I gradually reduce the diameter of the circle while always keeping the horse in contact with the two walls of the corner. Throughout, I remain on the bisection of the 90 degree angle of the corner, which I mark with the heel of my left boot as I turn.

My right hand is close enough to touch the horse with the thong of the whip and I activate it firmly, using a high tone of voice: 'Trot on'.

The horse takes up a contact against the lunge line, trots forward rhythmically and enters the corner which it has been taught not to be afraid of. It then works round the sides of the wall on the 180 degree circumference delineated by the limitations of the corner. It will then continue on to the second half of the 6-m circle, following a free arc of 180 degrees. On the second half of the circle there are no lateral limitations and, therefore, there is a risk of the horse swinging its quarters out on this part.

I now make fine adjustments to the length of the side

Short lunge in the corner. The trainer walks backwards.

reins by shortening them where they buckle to the roller. I always keep the side reins the same length on both sides and also begin to make gradual adjustments to their height, beginning with the side reins attached to the lowest buckles and, after much work, changing progressively to higher ones, all the while seeking the best possible harmony of the position of mouth, nose, poll and neck. The ideal is to get to the highest buckle, which gives the side reins a similar line to that of driving reins running from the bit to the collar terret of the wheeler to the leader of my tandem team.

Finally, I work on upwards and downwards transitions from slower to faster paces on the 6-m circle in the corner. Selectively and methodically alternating half-halts and half-stops in the corner, and also stopping before entering it again, is the key to successful schooling on the half-length lunge, which must concentrate especially on suppling the side to which the horse is stiff. Most horses are stiff to bend to one side. It is believed that many foals lie curled to the left while in their mothers' wombs and are thus left-sided, which means that they find it easier to bend to the left and stiffer to the right.

Work on the short lunge

This represents the very beginning of high-school training and should only be embarked upon by a skilled trainer with a wide experience of dressage.

This training is difficult and involves working on two tracks. Its great advantage is that it will obtain a better bend of the horse through the geometrical figures of the dressage arena. Very few drivers are able to achieve the *ne plus ultra* two-track work of ridden dressage but their numbers will increase as drivers seek to win dressage competitions in international tandem events, especially performing dressage to music, permitting free paces and shoulder-in by the leader.

Conclusion

'The work on foot on the lunge and on the cavesson is intended to retain, elevate, render supple, teach to turn and to halt, as also to relax the neck and to bend the shoulders and to make them supple.' (William, Duke of Newcastle (1592–1676))

8
Schooling the horse – other methods

In a publication on tandem driving, it is not possible to give an exhaustive study of all of the methods of schooling, so I shall limit my explanations to a study of the problems relating to the lateral bend of the horse that is being schooled. This subject is well illustrated by the following two quotations.

> Lateral flexion is necessary in different degrees when describing large circles, changes of rein or voltes, so that the horse can execute these exercises not only with suppleness but also in perfect balance and with regularity. In the case of a school or dressage horse a slight bend to the inside is asked for, even on a straight line, so that the horse in the track must go straight forward with a correct bend.
> (Colonel Alois Podhajsky, Chief Equerry of the Spanish Riding School of Vienna, (*L'Equitation*, 1965)

The flexion is only correct and useful if the horse offers it voluntarily and does not need prolonged and violent action of the flexing rein to be kept in this position. That is why the rider must prevent the horse from leaning on and resisting the inner rein, not only by alternately giving and retaking this inner rein but also by frequent opposition on the outer rein. Blocking with the hand is the stumbling-block that lies in wait.
(Gustav Steinbrecht, Equerry of the Seegerhof in Berlin, *Das Gymnasium des Pferdes*, 1865)

The principles contained in these two quotations will be examined further in the sections on long-reining and riding and driving in single harness and then again in the chapter on handling the reins of a driven tandem.

Training the horse in long-reins

In long-reining, the horse wears a bit to which two long-reins are attached, and is then worked by the trainer on foot. Some people also refer to long-reins as double lungeing reins.

Using long-reins

A very early reference to long-reining, dating from the beginning of this century, is given by the Marquis de Mauleon. Non-commissioned officers of the French Army were expected to obey the following guidelines: 'The non-commissioned officers will engage in the rather forceful exercises which this method requires ... a mechanical effort based rather on profession than on Art ... uses a certain amount of force which excludes methods calling for delicacy ...' (*Méthode de dressage*). There is no doubt that the handling of long-reins in Saumur nowadays follows completely different principles.

In the German Achenbach method, the long-reins pass through the terrets of a pad and a collar, as described in *Anspannen und Fahren*. This promotes delicacy of feel and emphasises two principles.

1. 'The direction of the reins imposed by the two rings of the collar as well as the two rings of the pad is a fundamental and unavoidable necessity ...' This is less true today.
2. The direction of the two rings of the pad fixed at the bottom of the surcingle must allow the reins to be horizontally taut between the rings and the hand of the trainer on foot. Thus the two reins will support the horse's hindquarters through their contact against the outside of the thigh or hock when the trainer is no longer directly behind the horse or when the horse is working on a circle.

Nowadays, trainers find that there are two serious disadvantages in using this method. It is very difficult to achieve a precise contact with the horse's mouth because each rein passes through two rings that are set apart and the contact with the outer rein, when the horse is travelling on a curve, creates a counter-effect to that desired.

I have very little personal experience of the modern school, which involves the use of a surcingle but no collar. There is always a certain risk in schooling in long-reins, which can steer but can also restrain.

A comparison of exercises on the lunge and in long-reins without a collar

On the lunge
- If the side reins are correctly adjusted and not too taut, there is a direct effect on the nose without restraint.
- The action is regular and the bend remains constant if the lunge line is taut.
- Constant support is provided by the firm, outer side rein and counter-flexion is impossible.
- Halts and half-halts can be achieved without applying excessive force.
- It is not possible to drive the horse forward and restrain it at the same time.
- Good impulsion can be created through easy whip handling.
- Supple paces without any cramping can be achieved.

However:
- The use of the short lunge is very difficult and may be dangerous, so it is better to use a long or half-length lunge.
- Rein-back is impossible.

Conclusion: This is a simple schooling method that can be employed by most people.

In long-reins
- Unwanted restraint may sometimes be imposed on the horse through indirect action on the bit.
- The horse may show irregular action caused by intermittant lateral flexion resulting from the action of the reins on the bit.
- The outer rein does not give constant support and counter-flexion is possible.
- Halt and half-halt are dangerous on a circle as they depend more or less on the use of the flexed outer rein against the horse's outside thigh.
- It is possible to send the horse on and restrain it at the

Driving a tandem on foot in long reins.

same time, which could prove disastrous.
- Impulsion is less well regulated as the whip is more awkward to handle and the rein on the whip side must be put into the other hand to allow easy use of the whip.
- The horse's paces may become rigid and cramped.

However:
- The use of shortened long-reins is easier.
- It is very useful in teaching rein-back.

Conclusion: Long-reining is better left to very experienced trainers.

The combined effect of the two reins in long-reining

In long-reining, the trainer asks for forward movement with the voice or whip, or both, and, at the same time, also restrains through contact with the reins on the mouth of a sensitive and forward-going horse. My reservations about the use of long-reins are due to the fact that I have myself made mistakes when using them, which makes me feel that either long-reining is much more difficult than using a half-length lunge line or that I, myself, am not skilful enough in handling long-reins.

Having said this, I have not entirely abandoned the use of long-reins and take great pride in being able to drive my two tandem horses, in line and in long-reins, on a 10-m circle at working trot in the courtyard of my house. If you wish to try this yourself, however, I recommend that you do so in an enclosed area as they did escape from me once with fairly hair-raising results!

Schooling the ridden horse

Nuno Oliveira always said: 'A horse at school must always be bridled with a jointed snaffle, from breaking in up to elementary schooling as well as for pirouette, piaffe and passage. The double bridle with its curb is only used to finish the horse in collection. The snaffle gives the direction and begins the collection which is only finished with the curb bridle.'

If the tandem driver can ride, it is worth the effort of improving his or her riding by taking lessons in elementary dressage. In this way, he or she will acquire a basic understanding of the principles of the exercises taught to a ridden horse. This will be of enormous advantage in producing a correct driving turnout in tandem dressage competitions.

Here I am concerned with creating the correct bend of the ridden horse. This is obtained through the combined and harmonious action of the rider's hands, seat and legs.

The action of the hand on the side of lateral flexion

The inside hand achieves the bend of the neck on the inner side. This hand must act on a direct rein with a good contact to produce the required flexion. A hand that is too close to the neck or which touches the neck, holding the rein against it, creates undesirable pressure which unbalances the horse's shoulders and distorts the carriage of the neck. This becomes all the more important in driving when the rein is always a direct rein which passes through the terret on the collar.

The outside hand, which provides support on the outside (convex) side of the neck, is the all-important hand of opposition, which supports the horse and prevents it from falling in through the inside shoulder.

The ideal balance between the hands is perfectly described by Gustav Steinbrecht: 'Take and give with the inner rein and vary the resistance of the outer rein for half-halts or halts as used on the lunge or the long-reins' (*Das Gymnasium des Pferdes*).

The action of the leg on the side of lateral flexion

The inside leg is held permanently and firmly on the girth. This is the pivot around which the horse's body bends. If the inner leg goes behind the girth, it makes the hindquarters swing out, which is to be avoided. The outside leg should be positioned a few centimetres behind the girth to prevent the hindquarters from swinging out.

The action of the seat

The seat is the part of the rider's body that is in contact with the saddle. An X-ray of a rider's pelvis in the saddle (as shown in the illustration) shows the two seat bones (*i* for the Latin word *ischium*). When sitting correctly in the saddle, the rider rests his or her weight equally on both seat bones. When the horse bends, however, the rider

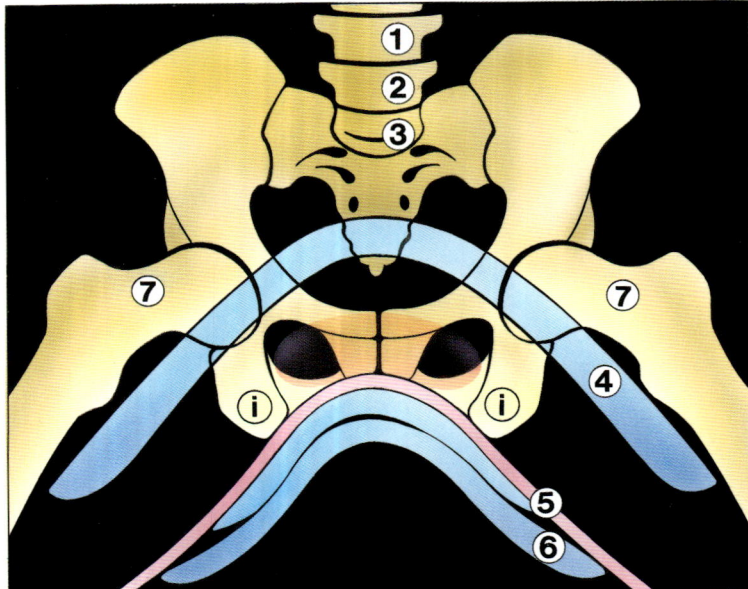

The rider's seat. The seatbones are indicated by the letter i.

must place more weight on the inner seat bone without leaning in to one side or out to the other, which is one of the worst things a rider can do.

Conclusion

When schooling a horse under saddle that is destined for tandem driving, the rider's final aim is to create a bend without the use of legs or seat and he or she must work progressively towards this by ceasing to give the aids with legs or seat once the horse has been sufficiently well trained to respond to all the ridden aids for bending. The more delicate and exact the actions of the rider become, the more sensitive the driving horse will become to the isolated action of the inner, bending, rein and the outer, supporting, rein as held by the driver.

Schooling the driven horse in single harness

Before one can begin the serious training of a horse in single harness, with the eventual aim of driving it in tandem, it is obviously essential to understand the basic principles involved.

When harnessed to a two-wheeled carriage, the degree to which the wheeler can bend is limited by the shafts. These do not confine the horse's body totally, however, as the neck may bend easily and freely and it is also possible for the horse to swing its hindquarters out.

Whereas in the ridden horse, the legs and seat of the rider would prevent the quarters from swinging out, in the driven horse the whip fulfils this function. To keep the quarters in the correct position, the driver will gently touch the horse's thigh with the end of the stick or, even better, the double thong of a tandem training whip.

If you study the illustration of an English gentleman driving his horse at a good pace, you will see that he has a lateral flexion of the horse's neck as he prepares to turn right and that he is 'analysing the turn' by looking to the right, as his girl groom does also. The reins are semi-taut, which shows that he is giving and taking the inner rein. This gentleman may not have read all the right books on driving but, none the less, he is doing exactly what is necessary to turn a horse in single harness.

For tandem driving, both the wheeler and the leader should be worked in this fashion in a dressage arena, going

Perfect English single driving.

through all the possible school figures with absolute accuracy and ensuring that the horse always bends to the correct side by using a flexing inner rein supported by the outside rein. If the horses are destined to be driven in tandem driving trials, as soon as possible in their training they must be driven singly through the countryside and through cones and other obstacles.

It is possible to begin driving a tandem team without having ridden the horses but it is quite out of the question even to contemplate attempting to drive a tandem if one does not have a perfect knowledge of the fundamental discipline of driving a single turnout.

Epilogue

> A well-chosen carriage horse ... well deserves the two basic qualities of any trained horse, viz., suppleness and obedience ...

The horse should first be trotted on the lunge, then mounted and put on the shoulder-in to curve it, impart a handsome posture and give it good contact. It should also learn to pass its legs one over the other in the croup to the wall ... it must be able to pass one leg over the other, both fore and hind, without which ability it will stumble, drag the haunches or turn clumsily ...

Another thing rarely taught, but which every carriage horse should show, is a slight curve towards the side on which it travels ... This posture augments the grace of a horse which trots well, allows it to see the path before it, keeps the croup aligned with the shoulders, and keeps the trot unified ...

If anyone finds it strange that I prescribe the same principles for carriage horses as for those in the manège, let him examine the teams of the nobility who appreciate handsome equipages and have their horses trained before putting them to the carriage.

(François Robichon de la Guérinière, Ecuyer du Roy, 'Carriage horses', *School of Horsemanship*, 1733 (J. A. Allen 1994))

9

Driving tandems

The rein-handling techniques required by a tandem driver are so refined that it is necessary to give a clear and accurate description of handling methods here.

First I shall explain the three-rein principle of English tandem driving. This is used in Britain when driving four-in-hand and tandem teams and my best source of a description of this method has been the writing of Captain C. Morley Knight in *Hints on Driving*, first published in July 1884, and described in the Foreword of the 1991 edition as the British Driving Society's 'bible'. However, while the position of the reins is similar when driving these two turnouts, tandem driving does require a quite specific technique. In further chapters I shall also discuss other driving techniques as used in two-handed driving, one-handed tandem driving and random driving.

English tandem driving

Driving a tandem in the same way as a four-in-hand seems natural as the length of the turnout is the same, the whip is the same and the English rein style is the same. None the less, there are noticeable differences.

When driving a team of four, the two wheelers and the two leaders are fitted with coupling reins which produce a looped effect rather than a precise contact with the horses' mouths. The pair of wheelers are held straight by the pole which separates them. The pair of leaders keep each other straight by walking side by side and sometimes because a strap, which runs between the two kidney link rings of their collars, is used to limit their sideways movement.

When driving a tandem, things are quite different. The wheeler is held more or less straight by the rigid shafts of the two-wheeled carriage but the leader is held straight by nothing except the traces, which would only be effective in keeping the horse straight if they were permanently taut, which is not the case as they give an intermittent and very limited contact. The leader is thus almost completely free and can change direction with an incredible and sometimes quite unexpected suddenness. This horse is, in effect, only controlled by the reins, which requires a permanent and very subtle contact between the driver's hands and the leader's mouth. The slightest loss of contact by the driver will be penalised immediately by an error on the part of the leader, which will occur with such lightning speed that the driver has hardly any time to make a correction. Only the skilful play of the fingers will maintain a steady, light and continuous contact which will enable the wheeler to be driven immediately behind and in line with the leader. This is not an easy thing to do.

Before going on to explain the handling of the reins, I shall define:
- how to turn two horses keeping the wheeler in line behind the leader
- the exact way to hold English reins
- the use of English three-rein handling
- the varying positions of the driver's hands

How to turn two horses in line to the left

Imagine a turnout of two horses, harnessed one behind the other to a two-wheeled carriage, and moving forward rhythmically in medium trot. What do you think would happen if you simultaneously shortened the left rein of the leader and the left rein of the wheeler in order to turn left, while maintaining a light, still and constant tension on both right reins?
- The tandem team, which measures about 5 m (16 ft) in length, will turn through a large quarter circle.
- The leader will swing out to the left on to the circumference of this quarter circle.
- The wheeler, on the other hand, will make its turn far closer to the centre of the quarter circle, thus describing a smaller quarter circle than the leader.
- Because the two horses are trotting at the same speed, the wheeler, who has a shorter way to go, will find itself ahead of the path of the leader. The more the team advances through the turn, the more the wheeler will move ahead and to the left of the leader.

Remedy: The wheeler must be prevented from turning too quickly to the left and this is done by checking this horse with the right rein. The driver thus resists the excessive swing of the wheeler to the left by the use of the right rein which becomes the rein of opposition.

The amount of rein of opposition required depends on the severity of the angle of the corner to be negotiated.
- An obtuse-angled turn is simply a change of direction, not an actual turn, and the wheeler should remain directly behind the leader without any rein of opposition being required.
- As the turn becomes closer to a right angle, in order to keep the horses in line, a 'hinge' must be created between them through the correct use of a direct left rein on the leader and an opposition on the right rein of the wheeler. The result of this will be that the wheeler will follow in the tracks of the leader.
- An acute angle is fraught with dangers for the tandem driver. When slowing down to a walk, the two horses come out of line more and more and also lose impulsion as the reins slacken. In this situation, the leader can decide to turn round, therefore this manoeuvre must be tackled with caution and skill.

Holding English reins

I have written this book in English because English is the language most commonly used in driving and other equestrian sports. In general, I have used English terms and phrases in the text.

In the UK, traffic drives on the left-hand side of the road, which is called the near side. This is also the side from which one mounts a horse. The right-hand side is referred to as the off side. However, many people around the world talk about the left side and the right side and,

to avoid confusion, this is what I propose to do here. Throughout my explanation of rein handling, I shall use the following terms:
(a) left lead rein
(b) right lead rein
(c) left wheel rein
(d) right wheel rein

The illustrations should be referred to for the explanations below.

The left hand – the stationary 'pivot' hand
The thumb and forefinger must not hold the reins.
- The left lead rein (a) passes over the open left forefinger close to the knuckle, not over the first or second joint.
- The left wheel rein (b) passes over the middle finger.
- The right lead rein (c) passes over the left wheel rein so that (b) and (c) are held together over the middle finger.
- The right wheel rein (d) passes over the ring finger.

This forms the principle of the three-rein hold of the left hand. The left wheel rein and the right lead rein are held together between the forefinger and the middle finger so that the left hand appears to hold only three reins.

The reins must be gripped firmly by the three lower fingers of the left hand, so that they cannot possibly slip, the thumb and forefinger never being used to hold the reins except when looping. The thumb should invariably point to the right, and the forefinger be held well out.
(C. Morley Knight)

The left wrist is bent at an angle of almost 90 degrees, with the back of the hand facing forwards. The wrist must remain supple in order to adjust the reins and maintain a contact with the mouths of both horses.

The right hand – the mobile hand
This hand is always mobile on the reins, helping to manipulate them. The right hand uses three independent holds.

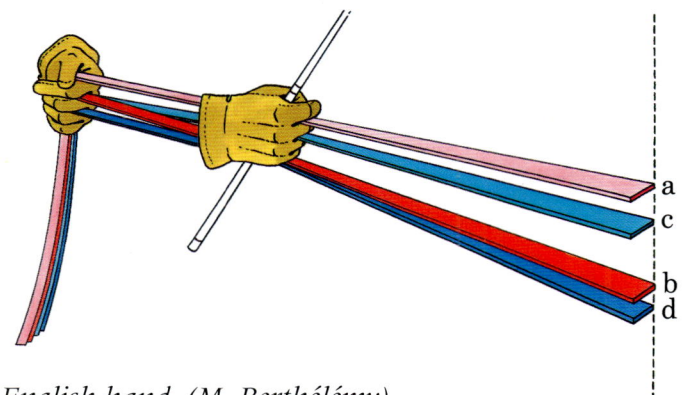

The English hand. (M. Berthélémy)

a		LEFT LEADER	L.L.
b		RIGHT LEADER	R.L.
c		LEFT WHEELER	L.W.
d		RIGHT WHEELER	R.W.

- The thumb holds the whip at an angle of about 30 degrees to the left and about 40 degrees from the vertical.
- The left lead rein (a) is held in an independent grip under the right forefinger.
- The left wheel rein (b) is held in an independent grip under the right middle finger.
- The right lead rein and right wheel rein (c and d) are twinned and held by a combined, two-finger grip of the ring and little fingers.

This forms the three-rein hold of the right hand. The right forefinger holds one rein, the right middle finger holds one rein and the ring and little fingers together hold two twinned reins which act as one single rein. By using the two weaker fingers to hold two reins together, they acquire more strength.

Crossing the reins

The right hand is positioned so that rein b (right lead) crosses rein c (left wheel). This has the advantage of steadying the hold on the reins between the driver's two hands and reducing their tendency to slip. This gives the driver a considerable advantage when compared to holding one rein under each finger as in the French full hold.

Using the English rein hold

I shall give an example using this rein hold on a horse in single harness that is trotting to the left.
- I hold my right rein firmly in my right hand, not allowing it to move at all and manipulate the left rein with my left hand only.
- If I shorten the left rein, the horse turns to the left.
- If I lengthen the left rein, the horse turns to the right.

In this way the English reins are shortened or lengthened to achieve the desired turn. In exactly the same way this principle is also used on the direct rein of the tandem leader and on the opposition rein of the tandem wheeler.

The rules for turning

Turning to the left
- Leader – shorten the left lead rein.
- Wheeler (opposition rein) – either shorten the two united right lead and right wheel reins; – or lengthen the left wheel rein.

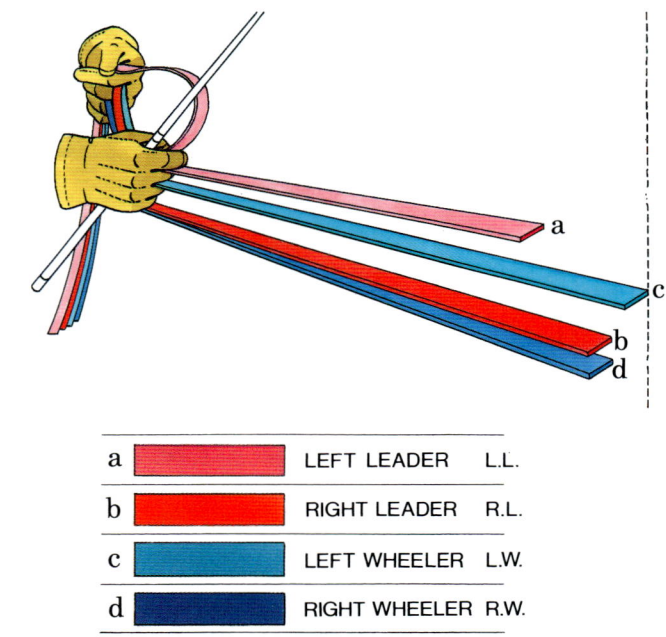

a	LEFT LEADER L.L.
b	RIGHT LEADER R.L.
c	LEFT WHEELER L.W.
d	RIGHT WHEELER R.W.

Specific tandem technique: turning left. (M. Berthélémy)

Turning to the right
- Leader – shorten the two united right reins including the right lead rein.
- Wheeler (opposition rein) – either shorten the left wheel rein; or lengthen the right wheel rein.

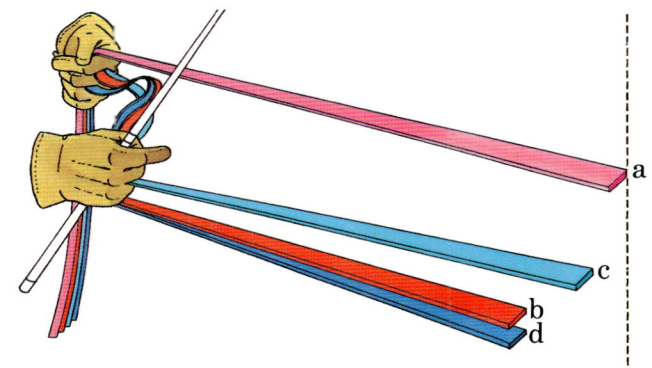

Specific tandem technique: turning right. (M. Berthélémy)

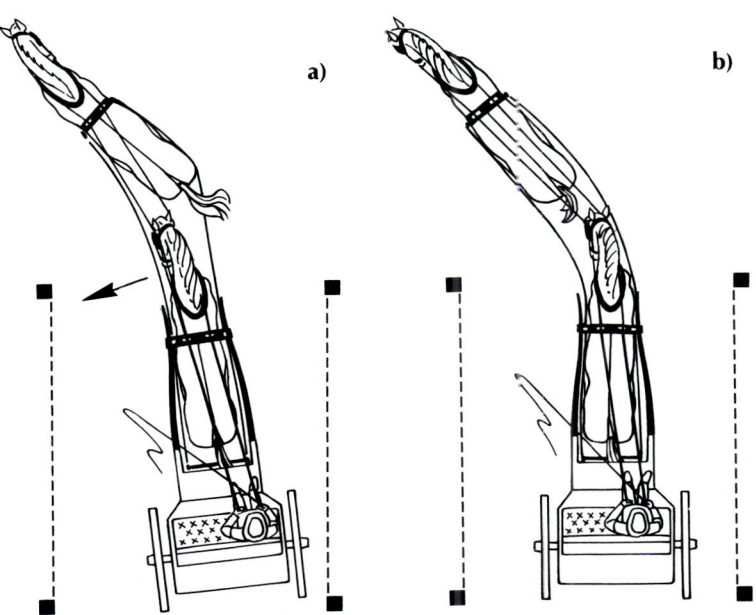

Left turn of a tandem, (a) without a point of opposition on the wheeler; (b) with a point of opposition on the wheeler. (M. Berthélémy)

The varying positions of the driver's hands

The hands can move in three directions:
- forwards or backwards
- downwards or upwards
- to the left or to the right

The left hand alone must constantly adapt to maintain a contact with the mouths of both horses through half-taut reins and by moving forwards to allow the horses to go on, or back in order to restrain them.

These movements are made possible by the articulation of the wrist, elbow and shoulder. Even the position of the driver's body can influence the tension and direction of the reins, a factor which is sometimes either neglected or exaggerated.

The art of English rein handling has been simply, clearly and accurately described by C. Morley Knight and I see no purpose in rewriting his words and thus running the risk of complicating matters. I shall therefore rely on his excellent explanation and simply add any clarification of

Twist of the driver to the right during the left turn of a tandem. His left shoulder is forward and upward as his head turns to the left. ('Crafty')

such detail as may seem fitting in order that the reader may understand, learn and practise the techniques of changing direction and turning.

Adjusting the reins

It is essential to be able to adjust your reins accurately when moving off with your tandem team. No one could explain this better than C. Morley Knight, whose description is of a team but can be equally applied to a tandem. Continental drivers should note that in Britain 'left side' and 'right side' are known as 'near side' and 'off side' respectively.

> There are various ways of adjusting the reins, either by pulling them out or pushing them back from the front, or by pulling them from behind, or by taking out the lead reins.
>
> • …The beginnes will very often find it easier to **shortening the reins** from behind by pulling them through the left hand. In this case the thumb and the forefinger must be used…
> • All four reins can be shortened, if much is required, by pulling them through from behind, but it is generally quicker and neater to hold the reins with right hand two or three inches in front of left (the little and the third fingers over the off-side reins and middle finger between the near-side reins), and then slide the left hand up to the right. By this means a perfectly steady pressure is kept on the horses' mouths…
> • **Both wheel reins** – It is better to shorten these by pulling them through from behind. This is necessary when going down steep hills…
> • **Both lead reins** – In order to shorten these, take out both the leaders with the right hand (the third and little fingers over off, and first or middle finger over near-side reins); you can then pass them back to your left hand the required length by letting them slide through and the right hand the necessary amount. To lengthen them, simply pull them through from the front…
> • **The two centre reins**. Always adjust them from front.
> • If the leaders are not straight in front of you, which will be found a very common occurrence, but are running to the right, they will generally come straight by pulling the two centre reins [very gradually and progressively] through the left hand from the front, so as to lengthen them a little; on the contrary, if the leader is running to the left, push these two reins back so as to shorten them.

Changing direction

When changing direction you are really following the line of an obtuse angle. The wheeler remains on the same track as the leader and follows along behind him without deviation. Both horses should go forward in an energetic trot and the change of direction does not require any rein of opposition.
- The left hand maintains a light tension on the four half-taut reins.
- The right hand manipulates either the two left reins with the forefinger and middle finger or the twinned right reins with the ring and little fingers.

Changing direction to the left

Open the grip of the right ring and little fingers completely and release the two right reins which will remain held in light tension in the left hand.

The two left reins are held and controlled by the right fore and middle fingers.

Resist with the right hand, carrying it to the left, upwards and slightly backwards to allow the team to bear to the left, following an obtuse angle and with the wheeler remaining on the same track as the leader.

Open the right hand to allow the team to straighten out spontaneously under the influence of a light tension in the left hand.

The right hand returns to its normal English hold on the reins.

Under no circumstances should the left hand be allowed to move forwards. It must preserve its role of 'pivot', maintaining a light contact with the team, which continues forward at a lively trot.

Changing direction to the right

Relax the grip of the right forefinger and middle finger completely and let go of the two left reins which will, however, remain held under a light tension in the left hand. The two right reins are controlled by the twinned grip of the ring and little fingers of the right hand. By drawing the right hand slightly to the right and backwards, you will simply allow the team to bear to the right, with the wheeler following in the tracks of the leader along the line of an obtuse angle. The depth of angle of the turn will be made greater or less depending on the pressure of the right-hand grip.

To straighten out, it will be sufficient simply to open the ring and little fingers of the right hand.

The right forefinger and middle finger return to their normal place on the two left reins.

Throughout the manoeuvre, the left hand should not have moved at all, especially not forwards.

Overtaking on the road

First, ask the team to speed up, giving a voice command and a subtle softening of the left hand, which maintains the contact.

In the UK, one must first bear to the right, overtake and then move over to the left-hand side of the road again. In countries where the traffic drives on the right, this procedure is reversed and the driver will first bear to the left, overtake and then return to right-hand side of the road again once the obstacle has been safely negotiated.

Because the driver is sitting to the right-hand side of the carriag, he or she will have a clear view of the right-hand side of the road.

The lateral flexion of tandem horses on the road

In the section on training the horse, I have already explained the importance of achieving lateral flexion of the neck while schooling the horse on the lunge, on long-reins, when riding and when driving a single horse, always insisting that two essential rules are adhered to:

- By alternately giving and taking the inner rein, you ask for the bend.
- At the same time, through gentle opposition, the outer rein prevents the horse from falling in through its shoulder.

While driving a tandem team at a bright trot along a straight road, both of the horses can be asked to flex their necks correctly to each side.

When driving on the left, as in Britain, the turnout must keep to the left-hand side and the horses should be asked to show a slight flexion of the neck to the right by alternately giving and taking the right reins with the right hand. At the same time, the team is kept on the left-hand side of the road by a resistance of the left reins with the left hand.

On the continent of Europe and in the USA, the turnout must keep to the right. This is done by keeping a contact on the two right reins to keep the turnout over to the right while, by giving and taking, the left hand asks for lateral flexion to the left.

The practice of bending the horses correctly while going forward at an active trot when driving on the road is of great advantage to drivers who intend to compete at tandem horse shows or dressage competitions. There is nothing better for encouraging a good position of the neck with a correct, slight lateral bend than active forward movement.

Of course, you must work equally on bending to each side in order to prevent your horses from becoming one-sided. For this reason, a solitary and fairly traffic-free country road makes an ideal practice ground.

Turning at a right angle

The spirit and sensitivity of the leader, together with the possibility that it will suddenly decide to change direction, do not give the driver time to loop the reins in the manner of four-in-hand driving. For this reason, there is a specific tandem driving technique for handling the English reins on a right-angled turn such as a road junction or the entrance to a street.

Turning left

The horses must be going forward in a regular trot. The driver must maintain a good contact, with half-taut reins. You must be able to 'feel' the horses' mouths with a supple left hand before turning.

The right hand Beginning with your right hand in the basic position, slide it forward along the reins, keeping your fingers relaxed.
- Grip the left lead rein (a) with the forefinger of your right hand.
- Shorten the left lead rein, maintaining a firm grip with the forefinger and letting the other reins slip through the other fingers.

- Shortening the left lead rein in this way will create a small loop in this rein between the grip of the right forefinger and the left hand which must remain in its fixed position – this is really more of a twist of the rein than a loop.
- The combined grip of the ring and little fingers of your right hand on the right lead rein (b) and the right wheel rein (d), respectively, will establish an opposition on the wheeler.
- The effect of the two reins on the leader is very slight because this horse has been asked to move to the left; the application of the two right reins merely prevents it from turning to the left too quickly. This will stabilise the leader and prevent it from falling in through its left shoulder.
- When making a turn to the left, it is illogical to begin with an opposition on the right wheel rein. However, if a tight turn is to be made, it is *safer* to oppose the wheeler before bringing the leader round.
- Please note that the left wheel rein (c) is not used. This rein remains neutral and is not manipulated by the driver's hand.

The left hand The left hand is the base hand and 'pivot' hand. At the beginning of the turn, the left grip must be fully applied, holding the reins taut. This is, in effect, a support grip. Once the leader has begun to turn, push the left hand forward a little towards the right hand. The left wheel rein (c), which is not manipulated by the right hand, is a neutral rein. This rein will slide forward between the middle and ring fingers of the right hand, thus lengthening the left wheel rein (c) a little. At the same time, I gradually hold back with my right wheel rein (d) and thus increase the opposition to the right.

Moving both hands together during the turn Moving the left and right hands together will aid the turn in a discreet but effective manner. Moving both hands to the right increases the tension on the left lead rein (a) and the left wheel rein (c) at the same time.

This movement of the hands is accompanied by a slight forward bend of the driver's body in which the driver lifts his or her left shoulder and twists the body to the right to assist the direction of the turn.

Finally, the two hands together constantly regulate the tension of the reins.

Straightening up The right hand releases the tension completely, leaving all tension in the left hand. The horses will then line up smoothly.

The left wrist is bent, with the back of the hand facing forwards, to maintain a good contact with the horses' mouths. A light contact will encourage well-schooled horses to go forward happily and spontaneously.

Finally, the right hand returns to its normal position in front of the left hand.

Turning right

The horses must be going forwards actively and into a good contact.

The right hand

Basic position. Slide the right hand well forward, a little farther than for a turn to the left. Start with the opposition on the left wheeler by tightening the grip of the middle finger of the right hand on the left wheel (c), and the backward tension on the rein will form a small loop between the right hand and the left hand.

However, the grip of the middle finger must adapt to the extent of the opposition required, this is *not a blocked grip*: the grip is loosened and retightened again as the hand moves closer to the body. The right lead rein (b) and the right wheel rein (d) are gripped firmly by the ring finger and the little finger of the right hand and this grip automatically shortens both reins. The right hand moves backwards retaining the firm grip by those two fingers on the right lead and wheel reins while the opposition grip established by the middle finger of the right hand on the left wheel rein (c) is progressively released. This requires a difficult adjustment of the fingers concerned for anatomical reasons explained earlier. As the right finger and the little finger of the right hand grip the right lead and wheel reins, *the wrist must be turned so that the back of the hand faces downwards*.

The movement of the right hand in relation to the left hand, which remains in its fixed position, causes three very small loops to be formed in the parts of the reins between the two hands. Note that the left lead rein (a) is not adjusted by the right hand and remains neutral.

(T. Coombs)

The left hand This is the 'pivot' hand, which remains firmly in position at the beginning of the right turn. When the leader has begun to turn, move the left hand forwards a little towards the right hand.

The left lead rein (a) is a neutral rein and is not manipulated. Instead, it moves forward on the left forefinger, thus lengthening the left lead rein (a). The driver applies a restraining effect with the right lead rein (b), thus inducing the turn. This lengthening must be gradual, however, otherwise the leader will tend to fall in through its right shoulder.

Using both hands during the turn The hands can contribute to the turn to the right by moving together during the movement.

Moving both hands together will tighten the right lead rein (b) and the right wheel rein (d) together.

This positioning of the hands should be accompanied by a slight movement of the driver's body in which he or she raises the right shoulder and draws back and lowers the left shoulder, thus twisting the body to the left to assist in the turn to the right.

Finally, the two hands, working together, constantly regulate the tension of the reins.

Straightening up Relax the grip of the right hand and keep a light contact on the horses' mouths with the left hand. 'The horses must respond immediately to the pressure of the driver's hand' (C. Morley Knight).

Ask the horses to move on and return your right hand to its normal position in front of the left hand.

Turning a corner in right-hand drive

This technique is used in countries where the traffic drives on the right. When cornering, it is important to identify as precisely as possible the moment when the leader must begin to turn.

Turning to the right

This is a particularly difficult manoeuvre because if the wheeler drifts even a little to the right, the carriage will go up on to the pavement. Great care is therefore required in making the turn. The driver must establish a good rein of opposition on the wheeler by taking hold of the left wheel rein (c) with a firm grip of the middle finger of the right hand. When driving a four-in-hand vehicle, the carriage is prevented from mounting the pavement by asking the leaders to begin the turn as soon as their forelegs are in line with the corner of the kerb rather than with the corner of the last building before the bend. However, a tandem turns much faster than a four-in-hand vehicle and the rein aids must not be given until the leader's head is exactly at the right point in the middle of the street into which you wish to turn. Only then can you straighten up the horses.

Turning to the left

First of all, you must look behind you to see if the road is clear. While doing this, the turnout must be driven straight on with the left hand only, while the whip is held out horizontally to the left, at the height of the driver's face, to warn any traffic behind you of your intention to turn.

A left turn should be begun a little later than a right turn would and the right lead rein must be watched very carefully to prevent the carriage from cutting the corner to the left which will happen if the leader responds too quickly and rushes the turn.

Only when the right wheel of the carriage is level with the right kerb following the turn can the grip of the right hand be relaxed smoothly. The leader and wheeler will straighten up in line as directed by the tension of the left hand which now takes up an even contact on both sides of the horses' mouths again.

Additional advice on turning

If the traces of a very eager leader should become too taut, you can slacken them by shortening the two lead reins with the right hand and placing a double loop between the thumb and forefinger of the left hand. The right hand then returns to its correct position on the four reins, to hold them as before. Once the corner has been turned, you can release the double loop.

This manoeuvre is also useful in modern obstacle driving.

Playing the harp!

There is a notable comparison between the tandem driver's manipulation of the reins with the fingers of his or her right hand and a harpist's use of the fingers of the right hand on the strings of a harp. The most vital factor here is the constant contact that must exist between the driver's hand and the horses' mouths.

This method allows the driver to maintain a contact with the 'steering' rein in order to indicate the direction in which the horses should go but also demands a contact with the outer 'supporting' rein. It is this contact which will prevent the wheeler from turning too sharply and will also prevent the leader from turning right around. The English method allows the manoeuvre to be completed when driving a tandem without removing the right hand from the reins, which is frequently necessary when driving a four-in-hand vehicle. In this way the rein of opposition is applied immediately to the wheeler without having to search for the desired rein among the four tandem reins which are all very close together. The handling is done progressively, smoothly and discreetly if the driver is skilful and has had the benefit of thorough training.

'The art of the specific tandem technique is composed of innumerable small, though most important, details, but probably no other class of driving requires so much attention to be paid to these minutiae as tandem' (C. Morley Knight).

Turning an acute angle at walk

(See illustration.)

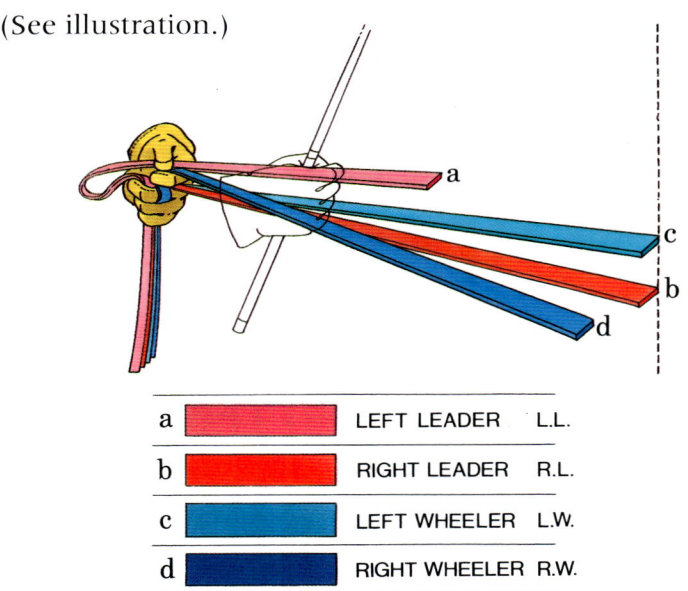

Acute angle turn to the left. Direct opposition, shortening d. (M. Berthélémy)

Turning left

Send the horses forward in walk, maintaining a light contact on the reins held in the left ('pivot') hand. The grip of the thumb and forefinger remains open. The right hand constantly manipulates the reins, which is why it is only drawn in outline in the illustration.

Opposition point on the right Begin by establishing the opposition point of the right wheel rein (d) on the left index finger. The right hand helps to place the right wheel rein over the end of the left forefinger.

Looping the left lead rein
- Slide the right hand 15 cm (6 in.) forward to take the left lead rein (a) between the right fore and middle fingers.
- The right hand draws the lead rein (a) back and makes a loop.
- This loop is secured between the thumb and forefinger of the left hand and the leader begins to turn to the left. Some adjustments will now be necessary.

Adjustments
- Make the loop bigger as the leader is asked to turn and adjust the opposition point on the wheeler during the second part of the turn by moving your left hand to the left, which has the effect of shortening the rein of opposition.
- Adjust the tension of the right lead rein to prevent the leader from wandering, giving additional support with the outside rein. Keep a firm grip on the loop between your left thumb and forefinger, maintaining constant tension

and thereby achieving a strong supporting rein: 'Do not deceive the horse's mouth' (Benno von Achenbach). Gently draw the loop slightly backwards.
- Watch for the moment when the wheeler passes the kerb or obstacle cone as it is important always to steer a course as wide as possible round an acute turn. If the horses turn too fast and seem likely to cut the corner, you must immediately seize the right reins in your right hand while the left hand moves forwards a little but without letting go of the loop.
- Once the corner or obstacle has been negotiated, allow the loop to slip gradually and release the opposition point held by the left forefinger. In this manner, the loop of the left lead rein is released late, which is essential as this loop bends the leader's neck slightly to the left. At the same time, it is imperative that you keep the right wheel rein taut.

In short, the tension created by the reins held in the left hand, the size of the loop and your firm grip on it until you have negotiated the obstacle are fundamental to making an accurate turn. You must 'keep the hand in the turn as long as possible to maintain the opposition on the wheeler' (B. von Achenbach).

Turning right
Send the horses forward in walk with a light contact on the reins.

Open the thumb of the left ('pivot') hand, keeping the back of the hand facing forwards and almost perpendicular. The right hand manipulates the reins and begins the manoeuvre by creating a rein of opposition.

There are two ways of creating a rein of opposition on the wheeler.
- By shortening the left wheel rein (c), as described by C. Morley Knight: 'The opposition is made by putting the left wheel rein round the thumb, passing it from inside from right to left, and then making the loop with the right lead under the forefinger.'

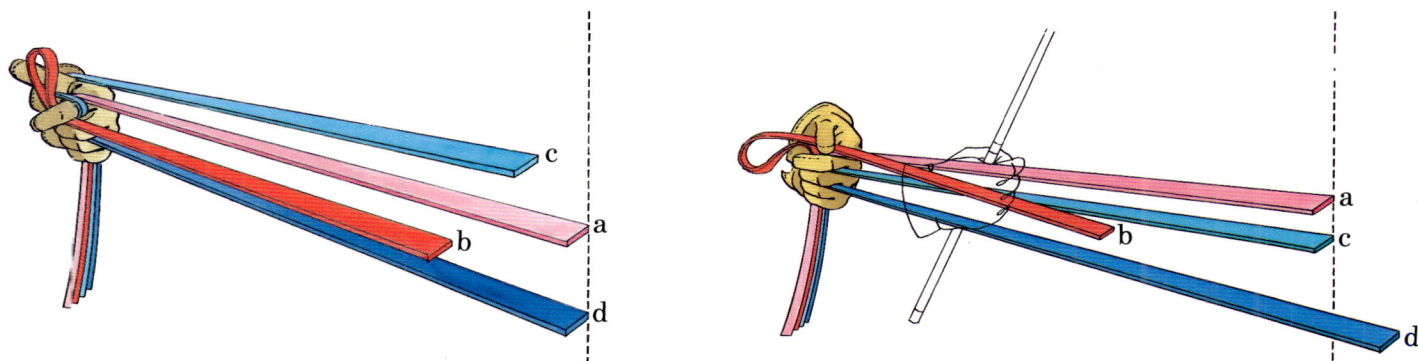

Acute angle turn to the right: 1. Direct opposition, shortening c. 2. Indirect opposition, lengthening d. (M. Berthélémy)

- Creating opposition on the left wheel rein (c) by lengthening the right wheel rein (d). Pass the right forefinger between the two right reins (b and d), then press down on the right wheel rein (d) and pull it forward in the grip of the right forefinger. The slackening of the right rein creates an opposition on the left rein.

Looping the right lead rein The right forefinger remains between the two right reins (b and d). This finger now reaches quite far forward to grip the right lead rein (b) and bring it back into a loop which is then held in a pinch grip between the left thumb and forefinger.

Adjusting the loop As the leader begins to turn to the right, you must adjust the loop in the right hand in order to get a correct turn.
- Adjust the point of opposition by moving the left hand towards the right hand as the turn is made. This increases the opposition on the left wheel rein (c). Sometimes I carry my left hand nearly as far over as my right elbow in order to support the wheeler with the left rein.
- Adjust the tension of the reins with your left hand to keep the horses moving on well.

Please note that, when turning right, the loop should be released earlier than when turning left. You should release the loop as soon as you see that the right wheel of the carriage has cleared the edge of the obstacle or kerb. If, however, you have lengthened the right wheel rein in order to create a rein of opposition, you must be ready to shorten this rein immediately to bring the wheeler into line behind the leader as soon as possible.

The reason for allowing the loop to slip later on a left turn and earlier on a right turn is because the driver is sitting on the right.

Further notes on looping for acute turns On certain occasions, this method of looping the reins must also be used when making turns of 90 degrees:
- if the ground slopes downhill, causing the reins and traces to slacken;
- if your tandem team is sluggish and the trot inactive;
- if the team is in walk.

The following method of looping the reins can be used to execute a U-turn at a very slow walk.
- A U-turn to the left is made by creating a point of opposition on the right wheel rein (d) with the left index finger and taking both the left lead rein and the left wheel rein in a double loop.
- A U-turn to the right is made with the reins significantly shortened and the left hand carried quite far over to the right to create opposition. As you turn, the right lead and left wheel reins are taken in a double loop.

During a U-turn, the right hand creates two loops which are then held between the left thumb and forefinger. The size of the loops is adjusted as necessary to execute the turn correctly. This is a fairly difficult manoeuvre and requires some skill and care.

Putting theory into practice

I have now described the three turns: obtuse angles, right angles and acute angles. The techniques used for executing these turns can also be adapted for driving half-circles and full circles in a tandem dressage test.
- You can make the horses bear to the left or right by taking up a small loop of the rein.
- By taking up a loop of the rein, you can take the tandem team round a right-angled turn in trot.
- By sending the reins quite far forward, you can use this technique to turn an acute angle.
- You can execute a U-turn by making a loop which you can then double or even treble if necessary.

When making turns using the techniques described above, it is essential that you take account of certain important factors, such as the paces of your particular horses, their age, obedience and level of schooling. You must adapt your expectations to the horses' temperaments, size, the weight of the carriage and the terrain over which you are driving. Despite these considerations, however, the fundamental rules of good rein handling should always be followed.

Points to remember

When driving a tandem through a turn, the hands must be carried to the opposite side of the turn in order to shorten the directional reins of both horses.

In contrast, when driving a four-in-hand vehicle, both hands must be carried into the turn in order to shorten the reins of opposition.

Driving on the road

The paces

The trot I attach great importance to a steady tempo in this gait and am always pleased if I hear the feet strike in unison. This happens rather more often when driving a tandem than when driving a pair. A similarity of size, blood and training is a key factor in obtaining this unison of tempo.

I always adapt the rhythm of the tandem team's trot to the faster horse, encouraging the lazy one with voice then whip. It is incorrect to ask the horses to walk too quickly as a way of activating the leader.

I take advantage of gentle downhill stretches of road to ask for collected trot because the gradient obliges the horses to engage their hind legs, i.e. to collect. I pay equal, if not more, attention to my wheeler as I do to my leader.

The walk With very young horses, I walk for three-quarters of the drive and adapt the tempo of the team's walk to suit the slower horse. I maintain a minimum contact but without letting the reins flutter at all.

I almost always drive uphill in walk and make the leader pull, especially if the ground is bad. This is a good training exercise for teaching the leader to pull when necessary.

Rein-back When I am out driving, I like to stop my team several times and I always rein-back at least once. When the horses have halted and are motionless, I take a contact on the reins, let the traces slacken, call to the wheeler then the leader and increase the pressure on all four reins together, continuing to speak calmly and in a slow, low-pitched voice.

Dealing with particular situations on a drive

Before a turn, I hold the leader back before I hold back the wheeler in order to slacken the leader's traces slightly.
- Before a hill, I encourage the leader to take up a progressive contact with its traces.
- On a hill, I slow down to a walk before the top of the hill if I don't know the road. When I drive down a long, steep hill, I hold back using all four reins.
- On the flat, a common mistake made by novice drivers is to have the leader working too hard. This is a serious error as it teaches the wheeler to be lazy and destroys the future of the team.
- A tendency to slow down is usually caused by the driver being too tense. You must drive with one hand only, keeping your wrist supple, your arm relaxed and yourself in a relaxed frame of mind.

Weather conditions

If it is cold, I wear a pair of silk or nylon gloves under my leather gloves which I purposely buy one or two sizes too large to accommodate this. In wet weather, I drive without gloves or wear cotton gloves.

If the weather is both cold and wet, I hold the twinned reins in both hands, which are carried apart, and I wear skiing mittens.

The ideal tandem team

My tandem horses, Phursac and Okapi, trot on in a lively tempo on half-taut reins which are held in my left hand with the back of this hand facing forward and the wrist supple. Without saying a word, I give 1 cm of reins, keeping my wrist relaxed. My team moves forward spontaneously and I then take up a little tension on all four reins. I can feel the horses take a confident contact with my hand and that they are moving forward happily with soft mouths.

The wisdom of C. Morley Knight

The following advice is extracted from *Hints on Driving*.
- Advantages of tandem: less expensive and less constraining than a four-in-hand with the extra enjoyment of driving a perfect tandem.
- The tandem is not dangerous if driven by an experienced driver, with horses that are fairly trained.
- Quiet horse, safe horse? No, a horse like a slug is terribly dangerous in a tandem.
- Follow the leader immediately if he turns suddenly and straighten the horses afterwards.
- The English three-rein principle simplifies matters considerably, owing to there being practically only three reins to think about instead of four!
- Always keep the right hand on the reins at night.
- Never pull your reins as if ringing a bell.
- If you drive in traffic like that of London, the utmost precision and quickness of handling the reins is required, please (1884 edition).
- A perfect tandem is driven with the pressure of the hands only: immediate response even if deliberately driven into a tramcar (1905 edition).
- To prevent the slowing down of the tandem, plenty of play from your wrist, if you please, the left hand firmly holds the reins but the wrist is turned in towards the body with the back of the hand to the front almost perpendicular.
- Right thumb and forefinger should be ready at any time

Phursac (entire) and Okapi put to my telegraph-springed cabriolet.

to take up and hold a loop of either lead rein.
- Left ring finger and little finger must grip reins tightly.
- Do not worry the leader, make the wheeler follow him.
- The constant use of the whip shows a bad driver. Try and work the horses chiefly with your hands, and to a certain extent by your voice.
- The wheeler should start the carriage.
- Never use the whip on a shy horse.
- After using the whip on the leader, quickly bring the lash into the cart and furl it later.
- The leader's traces must never be completely taut except when going uphill when the leader may be allowed to pull all he can.
- Tandem is admirably adapted for ladies who are fond of driving as their lightness and quickness of handling the reins are remarkable and surpass those of men.
- The whole art of driving is composed of innumerable small, though most important details, but probably no other class of driving requires so much attention to be paid to these minutiae as tandem.

A great four-in-hand driver, named Monsieur Dubey, an experienced judge and the co-organiser of the first international tandem event in Switzerland, sent me a most humorous quotation from Crafty's *Paris à Cheval* (1882):

> The tandem commends itself to a student of difficulties. The happy rival of Hippolyte [a hero of Greek mythology who died in a driving accident], this amateur distinguishes himself by driving a tandem in the outdoor school and takes advantage of the day when all the roads of the Bois de Boulogne are congested to demonstrate that one gets out of the most complicated and embarrassing situations with a little presence of mind and the manner to make use of it.

Practising English rein handling

Pulley
Four ordinary, equal weights hanging on four strings that pass over four pulleys will make a simple simulator with which to practise at home – with your eyes shut if possible.

Video
Another driver, who is a member of the Tandem Club Suisse, has developed a tandem driving video simulator – in reality no more than a specialist video game – in which the pupil sees on the screen what he or she would see on the road from the box seat of a carriage. The viewer holds and manipulates two sets of reins which influence the picture on the screen. In this way you can practise keeping the two horses in line, stopping, turning, driving along a street, etc.

10

Two-handed tandem driving

In 1985, I read a book written by HRH the Duke of Edinburgh, in which Prince Philip related his experiences of competing with his four-in-hand team. He wrote:

> For the purpose of driving a coach down a road the 'English' method works very well, largely because sharp turns are only required at fairly long intervals so that there is plenty of time to adjust the reins ... well before reaching the corner ...
>
> The problem of controlling four horses in the hazards and while driving the cones becomes much more acute. Many good drivers have demonstrated that it can be done with the conventional 'English' method but it is, without doubt, much more easily done by driving 'two-handed'. It may look a bit agricultural, but it works. In fact the Hungarians use such a method all the time. There are various ways of doing it. In principle it means holding the near leader and near wheeler reins in the left hand and the off leader and off wheeler reins in the right hand ...
>
> I have not tried to compete with a tandem, but I would estimate that it is the most difficult combination; in fact I believe that it is a form of masochism!
>
> *(Competition Carriage Driving)*

Until this time I had faithfully adhered to English rein handling while driving my tandem, but I now decided to try buckled reins in the two-handed method when competing at some events in France. I used this method very successfully in the marathon and the obstacle driving and was obviously not the only driver to try out this

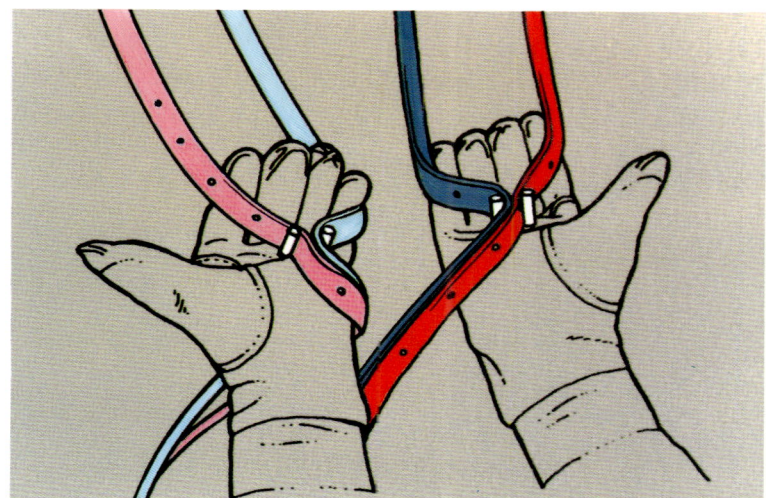

Two-handed hold recommended by Prince Philip.
(Competition Carriage Driving)

procedure, for, within the next nine years, many other tandem drivers had adopted this technique for competition driving.

When competing with a tandem in the Dressage class of Horse Driving Trials (Comipetition A), drivers should stick to English rein-handling techniques, but two-handed driving has proved its value in Competitions B and C, and therefore I shall describe it fully here.

Twinning the reins

Either two steel harness buckles or two clamps can be used.

Buckles

In the section on harness (page 24), I described the tongue which passes through the holes punched in the reins. This, however, can be hard on the driver's bare hands or even on gloves. Prince Philip suggested the use of two small steel rolls, 8 mm in diameter and the same length as the width of the reins. These rolls are held together by a threaded stud which passes through the reins, thereby limiting the thickness of the 'buckle' as much as possible. The finished result resembles the action of a pair of cufflinks.

Screw clamps

The use of these clamps offers the advantage of allowing the driver to regulate each rein with perfect accuracy while driving the course but they are inconveniently bulky. 'I know the clamps designed and made in Switzerland which are fully satisfactory ... for men of 1 m 85 cm [6 ft] with large hands!' (H. P. Ruschlin).

Buckled reins.

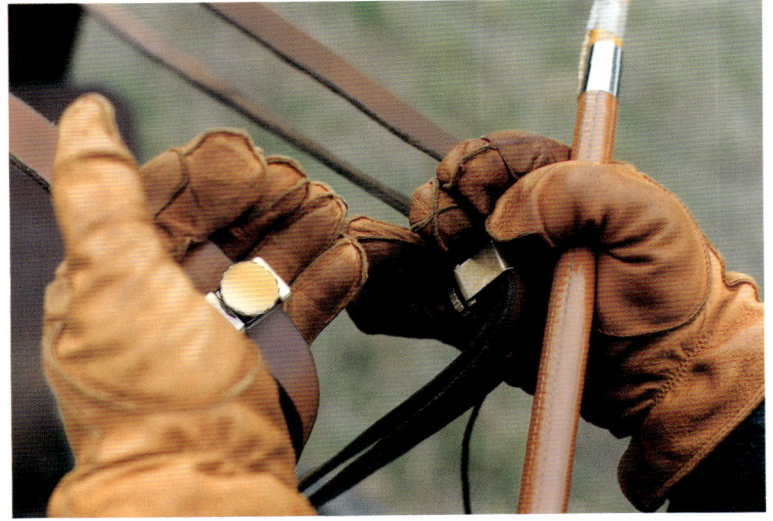

Screw clamps.

Holding twinned reins

The left hand The left lead rein passes over the left forefinger. The left wheel rein passes under the left little finger.

The right hand The right lead rein passes over the right forefinger. The right wheel rein passes under the right little finger.

The position of the buckle is either inside or, perhaps better, outside the palm beneath the little finger, thus allowing more precise contact with the tandem leader. The hands are held parallel and between 5 and 10 cm (2–4 in.) apart. The driver holds the reins almost as certain dressage riders hold a horse's double bridle reins, i.e. the snaffle rein over the forefinger and the curb rein under the little finger.

Making adjustments

From the moment the steel buckle or clamp fixes the two reins together, it is necessary to adjust each rein as accurately as possible. When driving a four-in-hand team, one can adjust the buckled reins from the box seat while the horses trot nicely along the road but when driving a tandem it is not wise to relax your contact with the leader, therefore it is preferable to adjust the reins while standing still. If the rein billets are long enough and have three or four holes punched in line, this will allow accurate adjustment of the length of buckled reins by a groom on foot. This is unnecessary with clamps.

How to adjust the reins

- The right rein buckle should be adjusted to be one hole shorter than the left rein (and the same if using clamps) because the driver is seated on the right-hand side.
- The leader's reins must be adjusted to be short enough to maintain a correct slackness of the traces.
- In a marathon, the reins should be a little longer in the cross-country sections without artificial hazards but all four reins must be shortened correctly, depending on the carriage used, for the hazard section.
- During a cone obstacle test, it is desirable to maintain a degree of elegance, therefore the reins must be adjusted precisely and neatly to keep the driver sitting up in a straight and dignified manner.
- The correct adjustment of the reins can be a decisive factor in competition driving and it is therefore very important to employ an experienced groom who will act in accordance with your exact wishes on the training field and know precisely what to do before the start.

The principles of two-handed driving

In this form of driving, two buckled reins are used, one held in each hand, with the buckle in the palm of the hand. Two types of movement are used, sometimes in combination.

- The driver moves his or her hands forward or draws them back, thereby acting directly on one side or the other of the horses' mouths with the left lead and wheel reins or the right lead and wheel reins.
- The wrists are 'rolled' when changing direction and creating an opposition.

Changes of direction and turns

Hold the reins as before with the buckles in the palms of the hands.

Turning to the left

If someone wishes to turn to the left when riding a bicycle, he or she would draw back the left-hand side of the handle bar and push forward the right-hand side.

To change direction when driving a single horse, the driver would draw back the left rein but rather than pushing the right hand forward would create a rein of opposition to the right to support the horse enough to prevent it from falling in through its left shoulder.

When making a change of direction with a tandem team, the driver must differentiate between the actions of the leader and the wheeler, therefore a different manoeuvre is called for – 'rolling the wrists'. With the back of the left hand facing upwards, the left lead rein is shortened to make the horse turn to the left and, with the back of the right hand facing downwards, the right wheel rein is 'held off' sufficiently to allow the horse to turn but still maintaining enough opposition to prevent it from falling in through its left shoulder.

Turning to the right

When turning to the right, the procedure is exactly the same only this time the right lead rein is shortened and the left wheel rein is 'held off'.

Two-handed turns

Everything that has been said so far about making right-angled or acute-angled turns needs to be re-read and adapted to the technique of using twinned reins. This is done by making loops.

Making two loops

The left-hand loop is created from the left lead rein at the base of the left forefinger.

1. In two-rein handling, the driver's grip on the reins must be modified. The English rein hold, in which the rein passes over the forefinger and under the little finger, is changed so that now the rein passes between the forefinger and middle finger and under the little finger, thereby liberating the grip of the thumb and forefinger of both hands.

2. The reins are lengthened by leaning the body forward.

3. To form the left loop, reach forward with the right hand and take hold of the lead rein (a) between right thumb and forefinger. Pull the rein back to form a loop which is

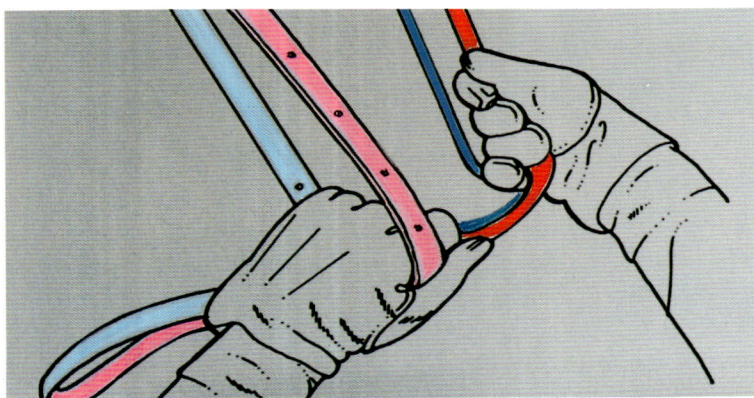

Wrists rolled: left hand, changing direction to the left; right hand, opposition. *(Competition Carriage Driving)*

Two-handed tandem driving

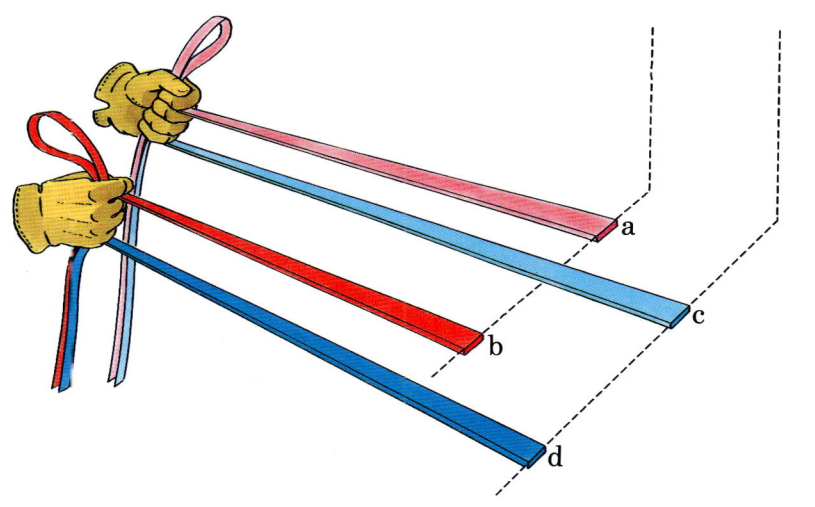

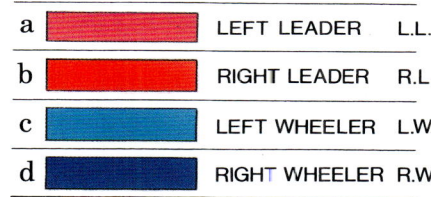

Two-handed loops. (M. Berthélémy)

then gripped firmly in the lower part of the left forefinger. This will take about two seconds. You must remain leaning forward slightly.

4. To form the right loop, take the right lead rein (b) between your left thumb and the tip of your left forefinger and pull it back to form a loop which is then held in a firm grip at the base of the right forefinger. This manoeuvre takes about two seconds.

5. The driver's body now returns to an upright position to restore the tension on all four reins. This has the immediate effect of shortening the leader's reins and, consequently, slackening the traces. The loops should be about 5–8 cm (2–3 in.) in diameter. It should be possible to make the loops in about four seconds but this time can be improved on with practice.

Turning left through a gateway
When the leader is nicely engaged, release the right loop and progressively begin to release the right lead rein (b). The right wheel rein (d) must remain taut in an exaggerated opposition to the right until the left wheel of the carriage has been seen to have cleared the obstacle.

Having successfully negotiated the obstacle you can now straighten out the team and carriage by releasing the left lead rein loop quite quickly. On the other hand, if you have been very skilful, only about half or even a third of each loop will have been released, leaving you with the ability to execute one or two further manoeuvres without having to make any more loops. This is obviously of enormous advantage when several gates have to be negotiated in quick succession.

Turning right through a gateway

The technique is precisely the same apart from the fact that, this time, the left loop is released first, the left wheel rein (c) remains taut in opposition and the right lead rein is released after the obstacle is safely cleared.

Additional notes on two-rein handling

- Making a single loop. When you are driving against the clock, it is sometimes helpful to make only one loop, then release this and make another loop on the other side for a turn in the opposite direction.
- The movement of one or both hands forwards, backwards, to the left or right is just as important as when using English reins.
- The combined effect of a supple wrist and the skilful use of one or two loops allows the driver to manipulate the reins very quickly and extremely precisely.

The disadvantages of two-handed reins when compared with English reins

- The contact with the horses' mouths is less subtle.
- It takes time to make the loops.
- It is less pleasing to the eye, lacking the 'qualities of elegance, beauty and harmony' that are so much a part of English rein handling.

11

One-handed tandem driving

Driving a tandem team on a straight road, using your left hand alone, is the best way to get a good 'feeling' of the horses' mouths. There are few things more pleasurable than driving in this way at a well-balanced trot along a quiet country road.

However, changing direction or even turning an open corner when driving one-handed is another story. This is an exercise requiring considerable skill and one which must be practised thoroughly in order to avoid problems with motor cars on today's roads, just like a hundred years ago when tandems were driven among other horse-drawn carriages. Obviously, one would not take a tandem out on main roads with heavy traffic and big lorries but it is perfectly acceptable to drive a tandem on quiet, fairly traffic-free roads providing the driver is experienced in turning safely.

On a straight, empty stretch of road, the driver will hold the reins in his or her left hand alone. The right hand holds only the whip, which is used to indicate an impending change of direction to other road users.

In modern tandem driving trials, the instances when one is required to drive with the reins in only one hand vary depending on the competition. For example, one is fairly frequently required to drive a 20- or 30-m circle with the reins in one hand during a dressage test.

Changing direction

When the left hand is working alone, it makes use of two types of movement.
1. The back of the hand faces upwards or downwards.
2. The hand works in combined movements of the wrist, elbow, shoulder and the driver's whole upper body.

Holding the reins in one hand

(See illustrations.)
To simplify the movements, the back of the hand facing upwards (pronation) and downwards (supination) is shown in the illustrations without the combined movements of the driver's arm.
There are three possible ways of holding the reins.
1. *The English hand*, in which the reins are held between three fingers, creates a slightly asymmetrical effect between the lead reins and wheel reins.
2. *The French full hand*, which was in fashion around 1865, was created by Count de Montigny. In this hold, the four reins are held between four fingers, which spaces them out more but also creates an asymmetrical effect between the lead and wheel reins.
3. *The Bill Vine full hand*. My English friend Bill Vine is

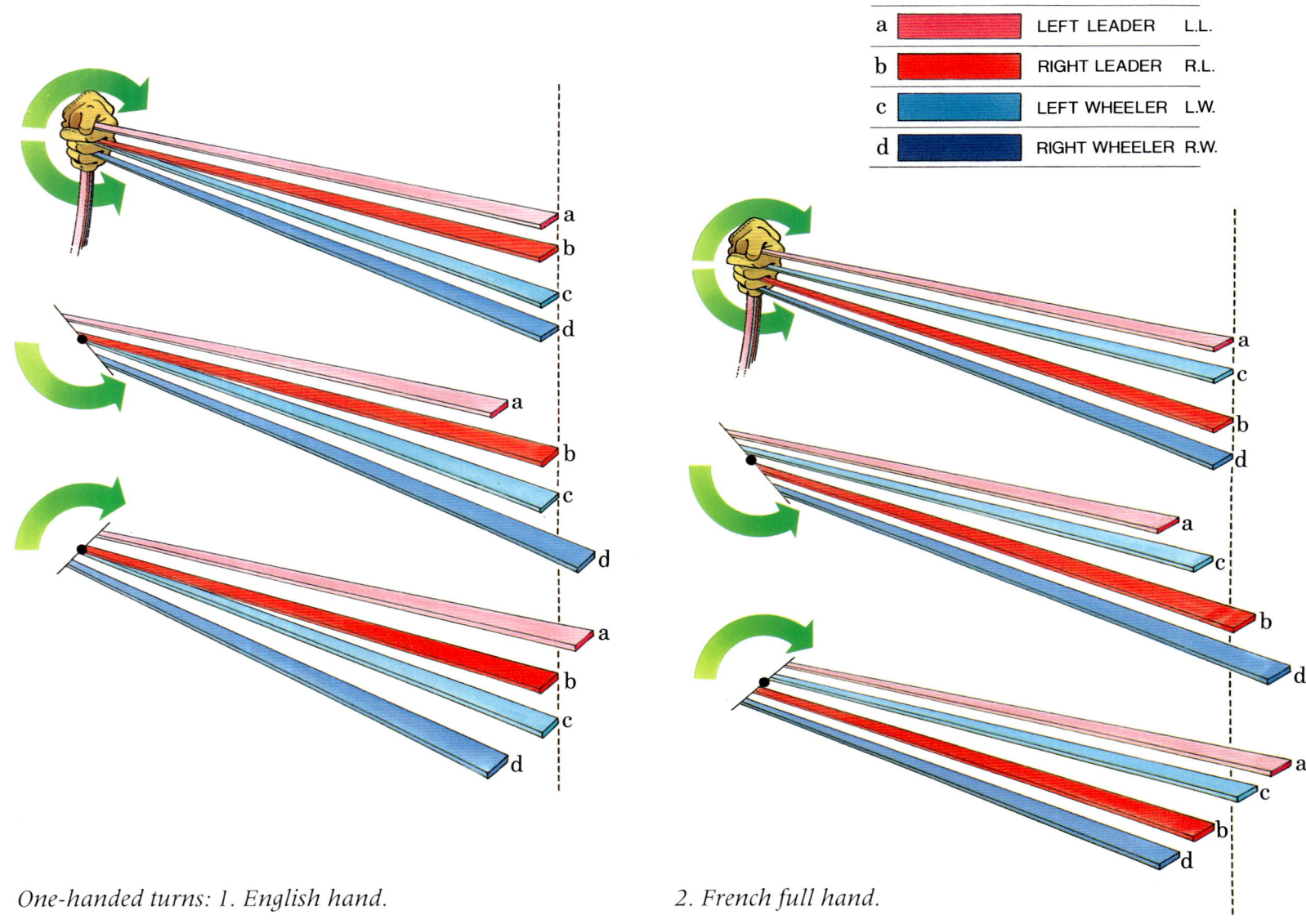

One-handed turns: 1. English hand.   *2. French full hand.*

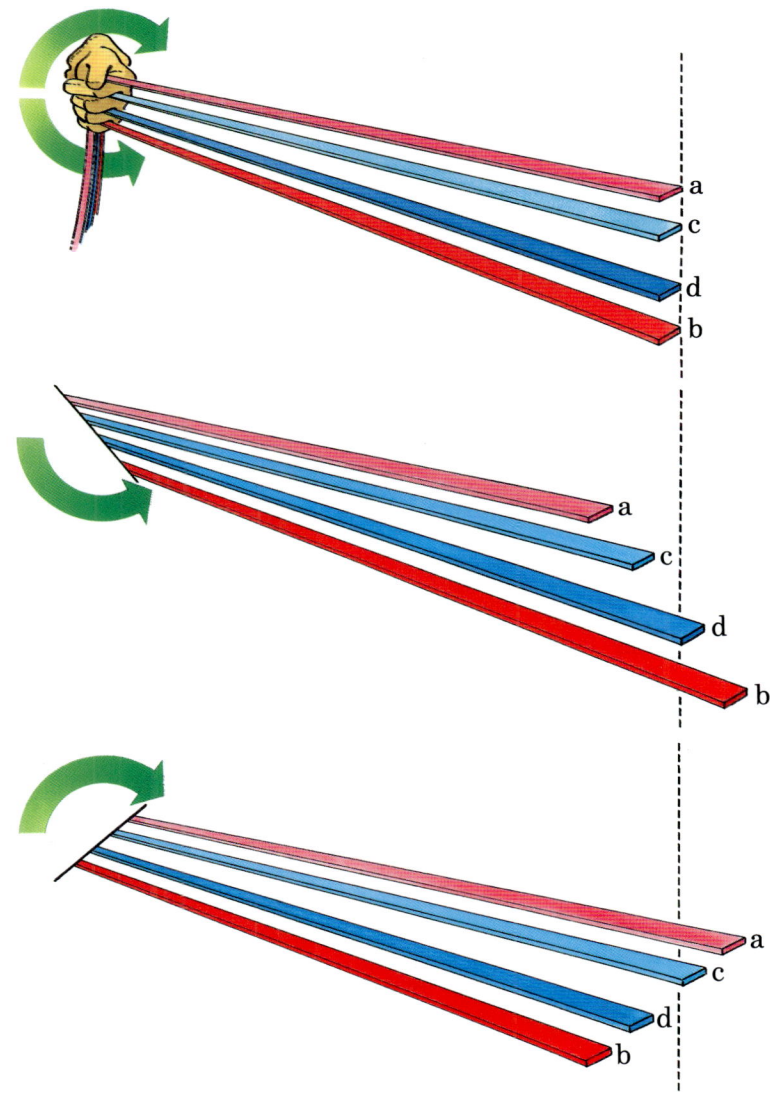

3. *Bill Vine full hand. (M. Berthélémy)*

perhaps the only driver who advocates the French full hand with the cry 'Vive Montigny!' In fact, he uses his own version of the full hand: left lead rein over the forefinger, left wheel rein over the middle finger, right wheel rein over the ring finger and right lead rein over the little finger. This four-finger hold gives a spaced out and symmetrical effect, with a maximum contact on the leader and a minimum contact on the wheeler, depending whether his hand is facing upwards or downwards. Bill's method of having the two lead reins over the fingers of the hand that are furthest apart gives maximum efficiency of hand movement.

At this point, the irritated reader will say that he or she has no intention at all of altering their way of holding English reins, which they have been handling perfectly well for years, in favour of a subversive Anglo-French full-hand hold solely in order to be able to turn the tandem with one hand only.

My personal suggestion is that you should just try the following manoeuvre. When you are driving, using the English hold as everyone does, please try the following technique. Use your right hand to remove the right lead rein (b), which lies on top of the left wheel rein on your left ring finger, and immediately transfer it into the grip of your left little finger, which is free. You are now ready to drive with a full hand and you will find, as Bill does, that you can now turn easily with your left hand alone.

This technique is very valuable for drivers who have to turn a circle one-handed in a dressage test. The driver has time enough to make a quick change from English handling (as described above) just before the turn on to the circle and, on completing the circle, the right hand takes the right lead rein again and returns it to its original English position. Trust me – try it and see!

Holding buckled reins in one hand

The most common reason for having to hold buckled reins in the left hand only is when the whip must be used, either to indicate a change of direction or to activate the leader by cracking the whip when passing a gate on a marathon or in an obstacle driving test.

The other time when you may wish to drive one-handed is when you are driving a tandem in trot along a straight piece of road and you do not wish to disturb the horses' rhythm by the small faults in handling that sometimes result from holding the reins in two hands, such as occasionally pulling more to one side than the other. Even if done for just a few seconds, this will result in a loss of balance in the trot.

- You can hold the two pairs of twinned reins in the palm of the left hand, with the left forefinger between the leader's and wheeler's reins.
- Alternatively, the left hand can also hold the twinned reins behind the buckles or clamps, which gives a more supple handling of all four reins and can even allow slight changes of direction by holding the forefinger straight and rigid between the left and right reins.

Finally, handling twinned reins in one hand requires the ability to make quite minute adjustments and, for this, clamps are obviously better than buckles even if they do look very bulky and heavy.

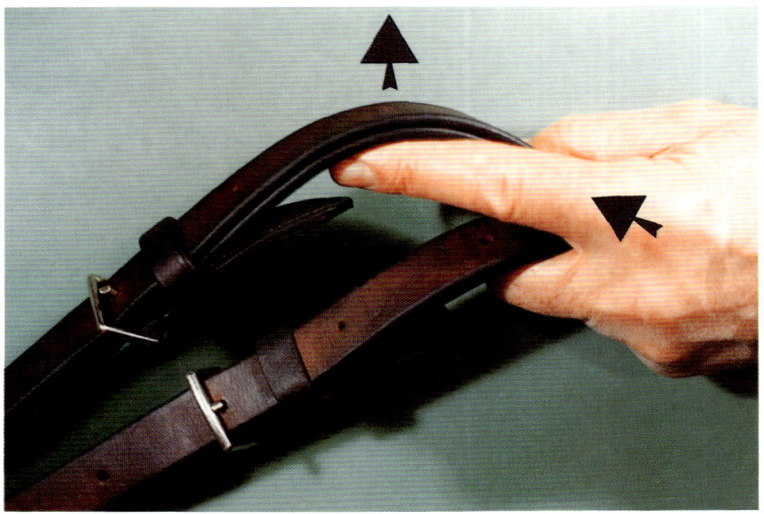

Holding buckled reins one-handed.

Notes on two famous tandem drivers

As a final word on my advice on tandem driving, I should like to say that although I have learned a great deal over the years through my own experience, I have also benefited from what has been written by others. Among the great masters, I should like to single out two whose wisdom I have found invaluable: Howlett and Achenbach.

Edwin Howlett (born 1835)

Edwin Howlett was the son of John Howlett of Norwich in Norfolk, coachman to the Marquis of Hereford. Thanks to his father's expert instruction, the young Howlett soon acquired an excellent reputation as a driver, which he furthered through his own intelligence and skill and the

E. Howlett and family, Paris 1906. (E. Howlett, Driving Lessons, *2nd edn, Charles Schlaeber, Paris 1906)*

ability of his own five sons. Eventually, Howlett was to achieve international recognition when living in Paris where he gave an average of 1,200 four-in-hand or tandem lessons each year! When, in March 1892, his book *Driving Lessons* was published, it became an immediate success.

A few years ago, I was lucky enough to meet one of his former pupils, a wonderful and very old French lady from Normandy, who spent a whole evening recounting to me all her memories of the master. I cannot resist quoting him here: 'When I drive I like to taste with my fingers what I am doing, and many people do not know the pleasure there is in tasting a horse's mouth through the reins ...' He was obviously referring to the use of English reins.

Benno von Achenbach's watercolour of a tandem, 1888. (Dr Jüg Wille, An Artist's Hand *(in German), Iska Verlag, Switzerland)*

Benno von Achenbach (1861–1936)

Achenbach received his driving education in Germany, England and also in France, coming to Paris to observe Howlett's skill. His most important legacy to students of driving is the 'Achenbach reins', also called 'nearside and offside coupling reins', which were intended for use in driving a pair or four-in-hand.

He outlined his theories of driving in a book entitled *Anspannen und Fahren* (Harnessing and Driving). However, this has never been translated from German and is difficult to read anyway as it is usually printed in gothic script (the most recent edition was published in 1988).

Achenbach reins are coupling reins and therefore cannot be used for tandem driving, in spite of what I frequently hear said in German- and French-speaking parts of Switzerland by my friends in the Swiss Tandem Club, who say that they drive tandem with Achenbach reins. In fact, Achenbach drove tandem with English reins!

> Oh, what a delight a Tandem ride,
> A high wheel cart and three inside,
> The wheeler steady and the leader free,
> If the Whip is clever it goes merrily.
> (B. von Achenbach, 4 June 1929)

D. Würgler with the handy new tandem whip which is easy to crack.

12

Randem driving

Harnessing an additional lead horse in front of a tandem team produces what is known as a randem in English, a *Random* in German and a *tridem* in French.

1. British randem drivers love difficulties! They meet through membership of an informal club and since 1988 to the present have competed annually for a randem trophy at Windsor, which has been won three times by Bill Vine.

2. The Alemanic Swiss randemists have a long and famous history. In days gone by, their predecessors drove six-in-hand in order to cross the Brenner and other passes to Austria and Italy. This remarkable heritage is the reason why they drive so perfectly today. (D. Wurgler)

3. German *Random* drivers compete each year at the Hamburger Tandem and Random Tournament, which is the last driving event of the year in Germany.

4. There are very few French tridemists but I was once privileged to see a nice presentation by two French tridemists who displayed a very attractive free-style show with their tridems, performing a type of pas de deux. (C. de Langlade and G. Sainte-Beuve)

The basic principles of randem driving

The horses
From rear to front, the horses are referred to as the wheeler or first horse, the middle or second horse and the leader or third horse. For a randem team it is best to choose horses that are already familiar with being driven in a tandem team or four-in-hand. The horses must respond immediately and without error to their own name, be of matching conformation and have identical paces and tempo when going forward in a good working trot.

The harness
The middle horse's bridle is fitted with two terret rosettes.

The carriage
This should be a heavy, two-wheeled vehicle.

The traces
One can choose long traces or two identical tandem bars.

The driver
A randem should only ever be driven by a very experienced tandem or four-in-hand driver who must know how to crack a tandem whip, as it is never going to be long enough to reach the leader.

During the winter, C. de Langlade likes to train the six competition horses of his four-in-hand by driving two randems a day. (1989)

Grooms

Two grooms are necessary when training as well as at shows.

Rein holding and turns

Holding six reins

The position of the left hand is exactly the same as for the English four-rein hold when driving a tandem, except that you now have the two additional reins of the middle horse – the left middle rein goes under the left lead rein and the right middle rein goes under the right lead rein. Furthermore, in randem driving, the right wheel rein is held separately between the left middle finger and the left ring finger.

The diagram shows the position of the right hand, which holds three reins under the ring and little fingers.

Turns

When turning, the position of the right hand is identical to that when driving a tandem team and the reins are handled in exactly the same way with the exception of a few, but important, details.

Turning to the left
- Create a slight opposition by pulling back the right wheel rein (d) which is isolated between the left middle and ring fingers.
- With the right hand, make a loop of about 10 cm (4 in.) diameter in the left lead rein (a). Hold this loop with your left thumb and forefinger.
- The right hand takes a second hold of the left lead and left middle reins together and you make a double loop, as shown in the old Achenbach illustration.
- The right hand shortens the two left reins together to make a progressive turn.
- To straighten out again, the right hand slowly lets go of the two left reins and immediately lengthens the right wheel rein (d) until it is back at its original length and tension.

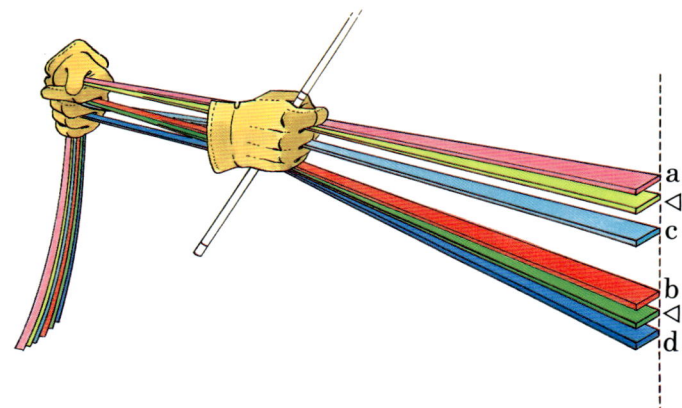

a	LEFT LEADER	L.L.
b	RIGHT LEADER	R.L.
c	LEFT WHEELER	L.W.
d	RIGHT WHEELER	R.W.

Randem rein handling. (M. Berthélémy)

Randem driving

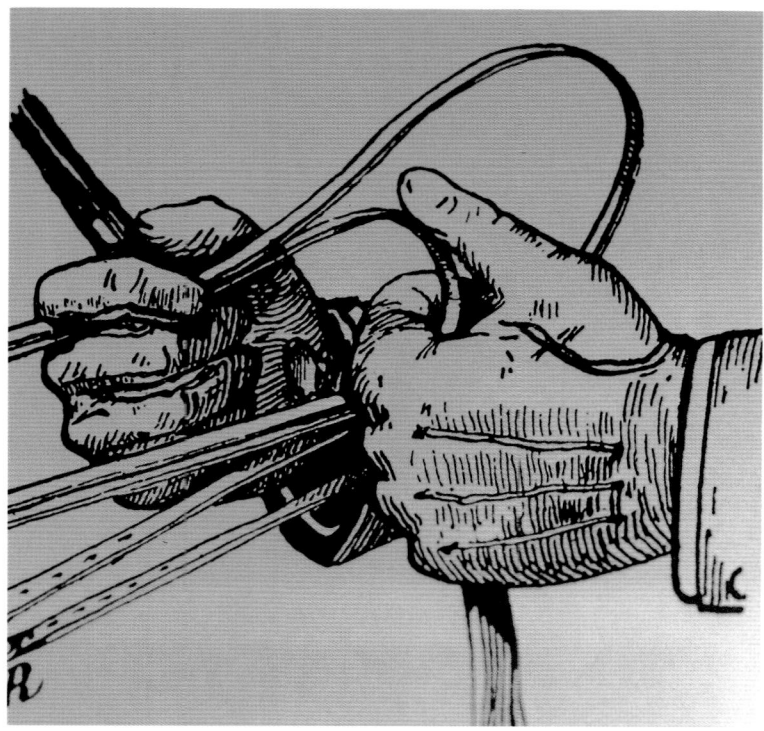

Randem left turn. (B. von Achenbach, Anspannen und Fahren, *Berlin 1925)*

Turning to the right This involves a similar but rather more difficult technique than when turning a tandem and I do not propose to describe it here.

Pitfalls to be avoided

- Badly or inadequately trained horses.
- A lack of discipline on the part of the driver.
- A sluggish trot or lazy walk without impulsion.
- Overestimating the randem team's capabilities – which are usually more limited than the performance of a tandem.

It is foolhardy in the extreme to attempt to drive a randem without undergoing intensive preparation on a driving simulator and receiving expert instruction.

13

FEI Driving Trials: introduction and dressage

Modern international driving events

In 1972, the first World Championship for international driving events in Münster used the official rules for driving competitions which had been drawn up in 1970 based on the rules for ridden three-day events. The rules for three-day events were drawn up by the Swiss founders of the International Equestrian Federation, which has retained the French title of Fédération Equestre Internationale (FEI). The basic programme is very similar for both riders and drivers over the three days.

Riders	*Drivers*
dressage	dressage
cross country	marathon
jumping	obstacle driving

The first four-in-hand three-day event was organised by the FEI in 1970 and took place in Lucerne, Switzerland.

Tandem turnouts have appeared only recently at these competitions. The rules for tandem driving are easy to understand because, with very few exceptions, they are the same as for four-in-hand.

The rules are revised and published every four years by the FEI. The current edition was published in 1993 and is written in English and French. Although this booklet sets out in detail the rules of the FEI governing driving events, it must be read in conjunction with:
- FEI Statutes
- FEI General Regulations
- FEI Veterinary Regulations

Anyone intending to enter tandem driving competitions must be fully conversant with the rules, statutes and regulations covering driving events.

Presentation

The *Collins English Dictionary* gives the following definitions:
- To show means to present something to view or to exhibit it.
- Showing is a presentation, exhibition or display.

In driving terms, 'presentation' describes judging the tandem turnout during the dressage phase of an FEI event. 'Showing' describes judging at various gaits. See Chapter 16 for the turnout of a tandem equipage for both presentation and showing.

Dressage: FEI Competition A

The object of the Dressage Test, Competition A, is to judge the freedom, regularity of paces, harmony, impulsion, suppleness, lightness, ease of movement and correct positioning of the horses on the move. (FEI)

To execute a perfect 'reprise de dressage',
To cook perfectly,
To make love perfectly –
All of this requires very careful preparation.
(N. Oliveira, 1972)

The important factors in dressage are:
1. the exact geometrical lines of the figures;
2. correct discipline in all paces and gaits.

The geometry of the figures

We shall take test No. 3 as an example, using an arena of 100 × 40 m (109 × 44 yd).

Scrupulous attention must be paid to the placing of the entrance gate, the letters and the marks between letters and on D, X and G. The judges and their scribes or note-takers must be situated out of range of the public who must not be allowed too close to the arena.

The driver should work to create good impulsion and rhythm in the practice arena before entering the dressage arena. He or she should ensure that they drive on a sufficiently long, straight line to arrive at A which will be a moveable letter that can be replaced after the tandem has entered the arena. It is absolutely essential for the driver to note and remember the exact position of X and G in order to halt the leader at the correct place.

There are six main figures:
1. a rectangle with two diagonals
2. quarter circles of 10 m in diameter. i.e. in the corners of the arena
3. half 20-m circles
4. one serpentine of five loops
5. one double circle of 20 m in diameter
6. two circles of 30 m in diameter

These comprise the *'figures imposées'* for the tandem team, rather like compulsory figures for pairs skaters in an ice skating competition.

The discipline of the gaits

The gaits and movements asked for comprise trot, walk, rein-back and halt.

Trot

Of primary importance is the cadence of the trot. It must be regular.
- The judge should hear it beating time like a metronome. The rhythm must be exact.
- The judge must see it on the ground in the regularity of the strides.

Once you have established the rhythm of your dressage horse for the test, you must never, ever change it, not even during a change of direction in the figures or in a change of pace within the gait.

Secondly, the driver must pay great attention to the three paces required in trot.
1. Working trot – this is a medium trot with a constant rhythm.
2. Collected trot – a short, higher-stepping trot with a constant rhythm.
3. Extended trot – a long, low trot with a constant rhythm. The stride of extended trot covers about twice the ground of collected trot.

Thirdly, the driver must maintain the impulsion of the trot. It is the nervous balance of the horses or ponies, expressed in neuro-muscular mechanical harmony, which allows them to maintain their stride.

In days gone by, a leader might have been quite a bit smaller than the wheeler but this makes a good dressage trot impossible so it is never seen these days in tandem dressage.

Horses and ponies must be very well bred to achieve good impulsion. It is also important, however, that they are sensible animals and not neurotic or too highly strung.

Working trot

The ridden horse
- The impulsion comes forward from the hindquarters.
- The horse's back must be horizontal.
- The movement of the forelegs must be light and balanced.
- The neck should be carried slightly upwards and the poll flexed.
- The nose should be slightly in front of the vertical.
- There should be a continuous and light contact on the bit.
- The impulsion is created by the rider's seat, thighs, calves and a mere touch of the whip behind the leg if necessary.

The tandem team
The driver has only a whip with which to back up the vocal command. This command should include the name of the wheeler or the leader, something which must be thoroughly taught when driving the horses singly.

The hoofprints left by the hind feet of a single driven horse or a mounted horse should follow the tracks of the front feet exactly. The hoofprints left by a tandem team in working trot may correspond if the horses' rhythm is the same and the distance between them is correct. It is therefore important to adjust the length of the leader's traces exactly.

Collected trot

To a judge of mounted dressage, collected trot is trot at its most balanced and refined, seen at its finest expression in 'passage' due to the controlled impulsion of the high school dressage horse.

To the judge of tandem dressage, however, collected trot represents only the very earliest stages of this pace. Eventually, as the training of tandem teams progresses, we may one day see a tandem team with the leader in passage during the sequence of collected trot to music in a freestyle competition. As a boy in 1935, I watched with admiration as the distinguished French driver, Monsieur Landrin, performed passage with his tandem team, Dublin and Portefuille, at the Grand Palais in Paris.

The primary features of collected trot
• Strong impulsion coming through from behind, with the haunches flexing energetically.
• The back should be 'lifting' slightly.
• The movement of the forelegs should increase in elevation and the stride should shorten.
• The neck should lift more, and the nose shuld be almost vertical.
• The contact through the reins should be subtle and light.

If you study the marks left on the ground by the hoofprints, you will see that the hind feet do not track up to those left by the front feet. However, the rhythm is the same as in working trot.

Extended trot

Extended trot is *not* allowing your horses to go faster. Extended trot involves the extension of the horses' legs. The hind feet should overtrack the marks left by the front feet.

The primary features of extended trot
• Eager forward impulsion which causes the horse to overtrack.
• The back should lift slightly.
• The action of the forelegs becomes longer. They gain in length and lose in elevation.
• The neck stretches forwards and slightly downwards.
• The nose stretches well forward and the horse takes a stronger contact on the bit. Pushed forward from behind by the action of the haunches, the shoulders gain ground and the whole foreleg extends and almost glides, level with the ground, until, at the end of the extension the foot is

Extended trot? No, flying trot! The author training for an amateur race, Normandy 1975.

raised imperceptibly before being set down. In French, this is known as *le coup de savate* (the slipper gesture).

If you look at the marks left on the ground by the hooves, you will see that the hind feet really overtrack the front feet.

Extended trot was first performed in mounted dressage competition in the Olympic Games at the beginning of the twentieth century. It had never been seen before this time in high school riding. The introduction of this new pace in dressage competitions was greatly influenced by General Decarpentry of France.

Some horses will perform extended trot spontaneously but many others have to be taught to do it. It is a pleasure to work with horses such as part Arabs, which, through their genetic inheritance and excellent impulsion, extend easily. Others, however, despite desperate training efforts in the schooling arena, never produce a really desirable result. For this reason, I shall give a fairly detailed account of schooling exercises intended to improve the extended trot. This training programme proceeds through four stages: mounted rising trot, mounted sitting trot, a horse driven singly and two horses driven in tandem. The lesson should be begun on a quiet, traffic-free road, not in a school or manège.

Mounted rising trot on the road

The use of the rider's seat is very important in obtaining extension. With the upper body straight, the shoulders back and looking up and ahead along the path that the horse will follow, the rider should rise towards the withers and sit smoothly. The stirrup irons should support the balls of the feet. The knees should be relaxed. As the rider sits, the perineum should make contact with the dip of the saddle behind the pommel. The rider must sit in the deepest part of the saddle. 'This seat ... is the only seat which allows correspondence between the centre of gravity of the rider and the centre of gravity of the horse' (N. Oliveira).

Diagonal
'The diagonal of the limbs on which you rise gains more ground than the other diagonal' (Decarpentry).

For this reason, it is desirable to alternate the diagonal every four, eight or twelve steps, depending on the feeling of the balance of the trot.

The preparation for extension obliges you to alter speed, which is absolutely forbidden in the dressage arena. As you change speed, you should seek and feel the rhythm that is best for extending. When you think you have found this tempo you should try to keep it. A good tempo for extension is the rhythm that you find when you return to the stables with reins half-stretched and an equal weight in each one until the horse tends to pull a little. Trotting in this manner side by side with another horse which already knows how to extend will have a good influence on your pupil. It is better to teach extended trot on a hard, dry road than in a field, which might slow the tempo and activate the elevator muscles in the horse's forelegs, thus encouraging the horse to gallop instead!

Mounted trot in the manège

Proceed on to a large circle in the manège and begin to ask for a more collected trot with good impulsion. Just as you reach the point of greatest collection, go on to a straight line, asking the horse to extend for four or five strides and then circle again, asking for collection once more. The best

Ridden extended trot. Mestro Oliveira riding Nairobi, Portugal 1970.

place to ask for extension is when coming out of a circle or corner and then pushing on down the long side of the arena.

Now try to increase the number of extended steps around the short side of the manège and then, finally, across the diagonal. Each time you feel the moment is right, push with your seat, maintain a steady contact and give the vocal command. If you use a clicking sound for collection, choose another sound, such as whistling in tempo or else shout out something like 'Yook! Yook! Yook' in a good rhythm.

Driving a single horse

Where I live in the French countryside, I am lucky enough to have access to a small, stone-surfaced road that goes downhill for 300 m (330 yd), is flat and sandy for the next 100 m (109 yd) and then goes uphill again for another 300 m. This gives me an excellent opportunity when working my horses singly. When going down the slope with the reins slightly taut, collection of the trot is easy and spontaneous. When I reach the flat, sandy zone, I give a command to go quicker but maintain a good, level contact with the bit. The horse can see the road sloping uphill again. Instinctively, it pushes forward from behind, leaning on my hand and straightening its neck slightly. Then it starts to climb the hill in a very active trot. The forelegs begin to lengthen their stride and, as the hill steepens, the horse increases the extension of the trot in order to avoid stumbling. Now the whole foreleg extends together – shoulder, knee and foot.

Driving tandem

I use exactly the same training method as described above and keep the leader pulling on the traces when going uphill. If you drive one-handed with a good contact through the reins, feeling both horses leaning on the bits, your wrist supple and the back of your hand flexed forwards, you will really be able to feel the two horses extending in line. It is a wonderful sensation!

Master T. Velstra (Holland) driving his tandem team at matching pace. (Manuel du cheval d'attelage moderne)

Tandem trot in rhythm

Once good discipline in all three paces of trot has been obtained from each horse in the tandem team, you may think of continuing your training in the hope of achieving complete harmony in the tempo of the two horses.

Two horses which are accustomed to working as a pair will easily become accustomed to trotting at the same tempo. When I ride side by side with my son, training the leader and wheeler of our team together, they really do like to trot at the same tempo. However, when I ride behind my son, although the horses are able to keep the same rhythm, they don't do so very often and are not always on the same foot when they do. A tandem team trotting in rhythm is one of the most harmonious sights to be seen in driving, especially in extended trot.

Tandem dressage tests

The competitor's main objective must be to maintain an excellent discipline in all gaits while executing the figures exactly.

Rein handling

The driver's way of handling the reins in a dressage arena is quite special. I have done my best to encourage the driver to manipulate the reins properly so that he or she can turn their tandem horses correctly by using the outer rein of the wheeler in opposition in order that the wheeler will follow the leader without falling in through its shoulder on the turn. However, matters are quite different in the dressage arena where the two horses are obliged to follow geometric figures in a small rectangle of only 100 × 40 m (109 × 44 yd). The horses are actually confined within this meagre area so that they simply cannot escape, just as when they work in an indoor school. The horses are well aware of the limits of the area in which they find themselves and will turn right angles almost spontaneously if you hold them straight and push them forwards into the corner. When driving tandem in dressage there is no need for the constraining brake of the outer rein of

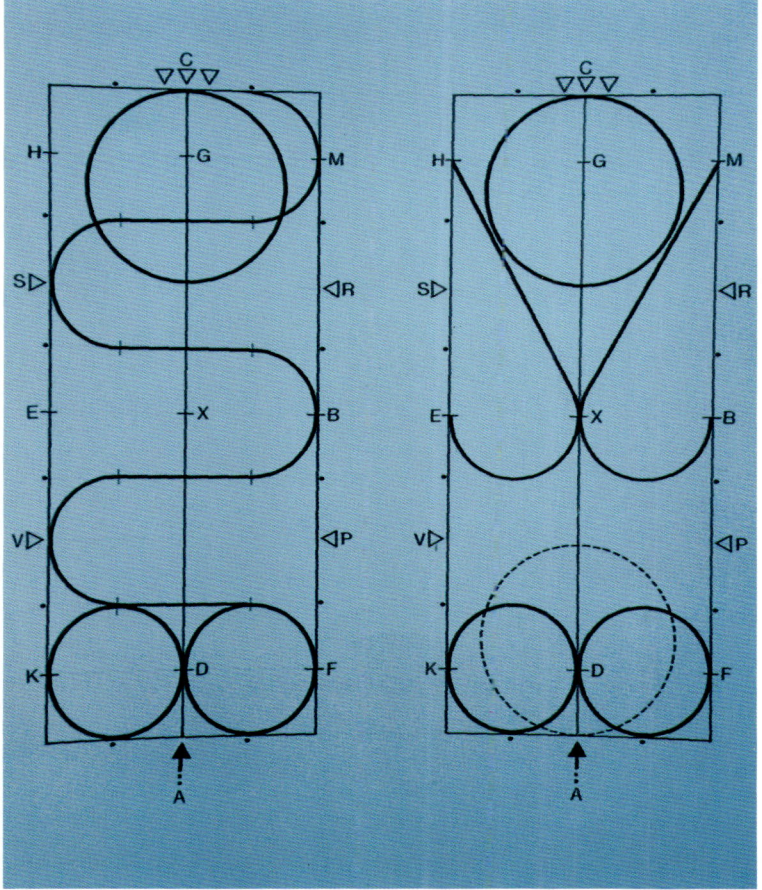

Basic figures of Dressage Test no. 3, advanced (FEI).

opposition that you need to use in wide open spaces. This allows good gaits to be maintained throughout the geometry of the figures.

The basic figures required in Dressage Test 3 (Advanced)

1. A quarter circle to the left when passing through corners

When proceeding down the long side, HEK, for example, the two horses will travel the whole length of the arena in a forward-going trot with their necks flexed slightly to the left. A subtle tension on the reins will keep the horses out on the track, thanks to good early training. On arriving at K, provided the impulsion of the horses is not broken by the hand of their driver becoming too restricting, the horses will turn left perfectly well without any rein of opposition being required on the wheeler. The leader should travel on beyond K and deep into the corner.

A driver's viewpoint

The achievement of a correct bend, slightly inwards, or at least the avoidance of an incorrect outward bend, is a matter of delicately precise rein handling. The technique involves indicating the direction of the turn by a tweak on the inside rein at exactly the right moment and thereafter giving with the outside rein rather than taking with the inside one. Provided the tension on the inside rein remains even and constant the horse (the leader) will reach forward imperceptibly to maintain contact with the outside one and turn his head slightly inwards in the process ...

The principle of giving with the outside rein rather than taking with the inside one is crucial to the proper execution of turns and circles in dressage. There is, in effect, a hinge between the leader and wheeler of a tandem which enables them to make turns and circles without cutting corners.

(Major Tom Coombs, private correspondence)

A rider's viewpoint

To turn the corner to the left, I push my horse as far into the corner as possible. I give a small feel on the left rein, push my right shoulder slightly forward and, twisting my upper body to the left, without turning my head, look forward through the ears of my horse which looks slightly to the left.

(N. Oliveira, *Dressage Notebook*, Lisbon, 1973)

The similarity of technique between the dressage driver and the dressage rider is clear but it must be remembered that turning a corner is an especially difficult manoeuvre for a tandem team and carriage of approximately 3 m (20 ft) in length, and that in Dressage Test 3 they are asked to turn a corner fourteen times in all.

2. Half circles and circles in working trot

This type of figure throws up another difficulty in that the borders of the circles are limited at only one tangential point.

Two half circles of 20 m in diameter

These figures ask for a little more than a half volte because the horses are not asked to follow on down the centre line at X but to go on turning as far as the diagonals XH or XM. Sometimes the leader is taken by surprise at this point because it expected to turn down towards C. The sign of a

FEI Driving Trials: introduction and dressage

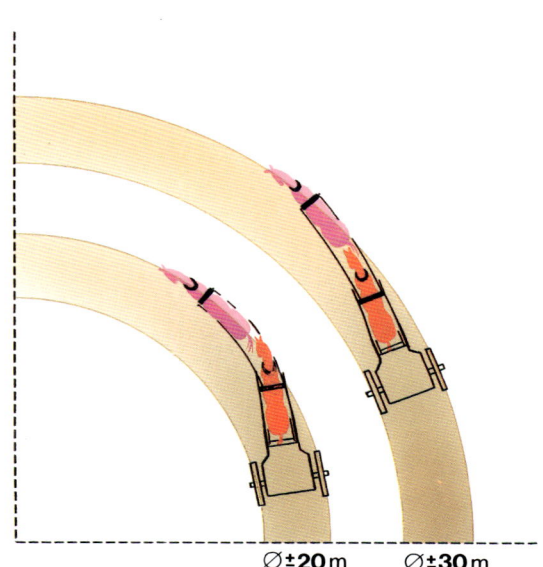

On a 30-metre diameter circle, both horses keep in line. On a 20-metre diameter circle, there must be a 'hinge' between the horses. (M. Berthélémy)

good line with a two-wheeled tandem equipage is when the route described by the middle of the carriage axle passes over the crossing point of the letter.

3. Five-loop serpentine

This is an attractive geometrical movement, with three half circles of 20 m in diameter to the right, plus two half circles to the left. The line is precisely delimited for the driver by five imaginary lines at right angles to the centre line, AXC. The movement will be driven correctly if the leader goes straight over and beyond the centre line so that the carriage remains at right angles to the line when crossing it.

The judge sitting at C will be able to judge the accuracy of the movement absolutely because, at the moment when the carriage crosses the centre line, the two wheels are exactly in line. If the crossing is correct, the judge will see only one wheel.

The route of the serpentine is very long (about 250 m or 271 yd) and it is imperative to maintain the impulsion and rhythm of the team if you wish to complete the last two loops correctly. It is essential that the driver maintains a light and supple hand.

3. Two circles of 30 m in diameter in collected trot

At this point I must say that to achieve collected trot from both horses in a tandem team that is driven with the left hand alone is impossible when driving this figure. What is important, however, is to remain on the circle.

When driving on the open road, it is a simple matter to turn a corner holding the reins in the left hand only, but an entire circle requires tremendous impulsion. The beginning always looks easy but then, halfway round, the horses begin to lose their energy and the circle takes on the shape of a rugby ball or a potato.

I have already described for the reader the way in which Bill Vine's one-handed technique will make a circle easier to drive. It is quite possible to change from the ordinary English hand to Bill Vine's method but returning your reins to their original English hold must be done quickly and correctly at the end of the manoeuvre and this requires thorough practice.

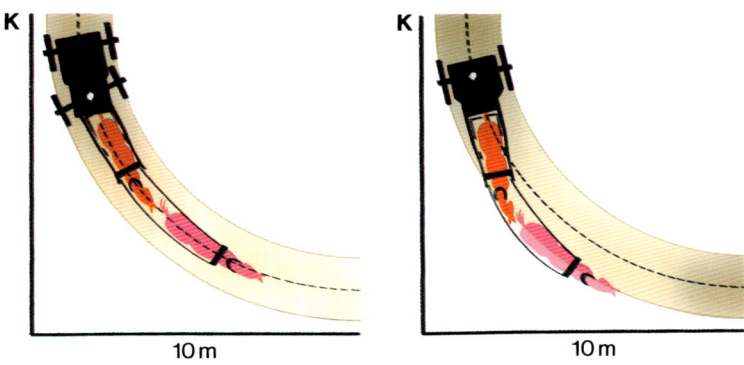

The position of the leader going through the corner in (left) a four-wheeled tandem and (right) a two-wheeled tandem. (M. Berthélémy)

4. A circle of 20 m to the left followed by one to the right, crossing at D – the 'double circle'

In movement 11 of the test, these two circles actually become two and a half circles – KDKDFD. Here again, the horses must be going forward with tremendous impulsion and the driver must have the hands of a god!

I recommend that you adopt the following course:
- K – send the leader on past the marker.
- KD – drive the leader to the right of D.
- DKD – send the leader to the right of A and only ask it to change direction after D.
- DFD – this is the most difficult part of the manoeuvre as the horses have now lost impulsion.
- DG – the team is now released from the endless bending.

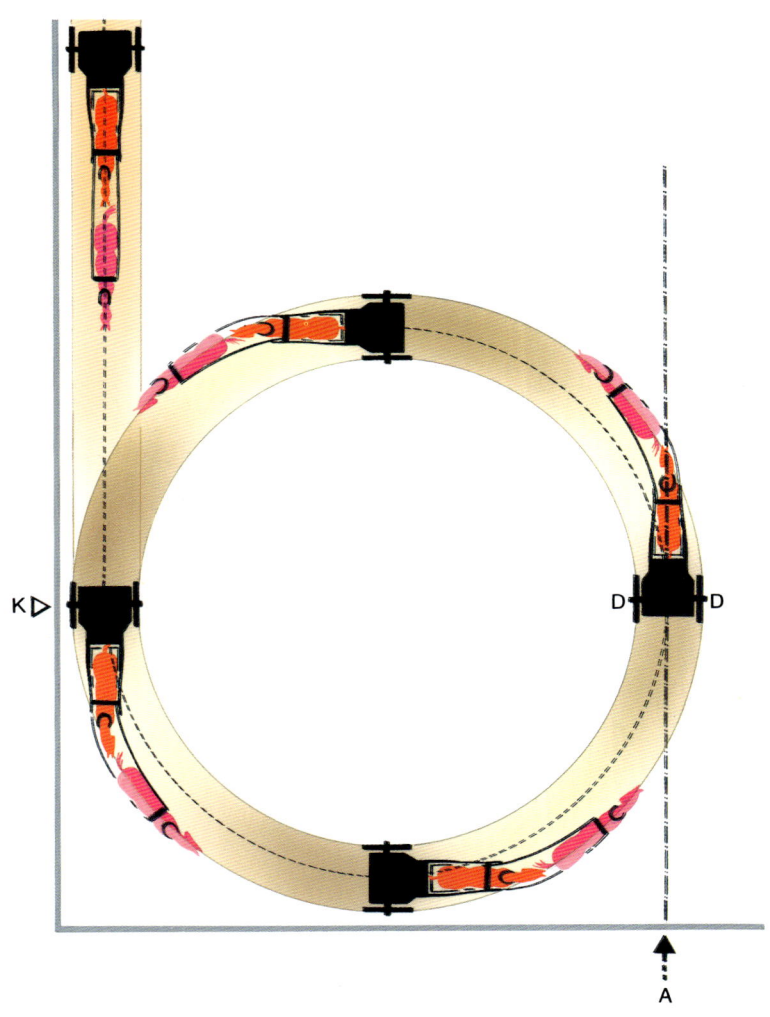

Tandems on the 20-metre diameter circle. (M. Berthélémy)

The horses will be happy to go straight and you may show a good extended trot to the end of the movement, with a good stop at G if you are able to visualise your markers correctly.

5. Extended trot across the diagonal
From the viewpoint of the rider I shall describe this manoeuvre across the diagonal MXK, using Nuno Oliveira as my reference. We begin on the short side, HCM.
- Approach the corner on the long side, arriving at H in balance and with impulsion.
- Along the short side, ask for croup to the wall at C to achieve collection.
- Before the next corner, change the lateral bend of the horse from left to right and go deep into the corner.
- As you approach M, the bend and collection of the horse are at their greatest as the horse comes in line with the diagonal MXK.

Now straighten the horse using equal tension on both reins, feeling the horse take up a contact and lean slightly on the hand. Then, seeing the familiar route of MXK ahead of it, the horse should extend in response to the aid given by your supple seat and vocal request of a few whistled notes or whatever your chosen command is.

It is a big mistake to push the horse forward in the extension and slacken the reins as this causes the horse to go quicker, lose its rhythm and bring its neck and head up – appalling!

From the viewpoint of the tandem driver The driver attempts to do the equivalent as the rider described above.

Well before the H corner, the driver should ask for impulsion with a voice command and a touch of the whip when training. This should activate the leader to turn the corner easily, cutting the right angle a little in order to maintain a good tempo along the short side to C. Do not try to collect the team before the next corner as they will lose impulsion. Go deep into the corner and you will find that you do not need to use your hand to restrain and collect the team as the corner itself will do this for you. Immediately the leader reaches the diagonal point at M, begin your whistle or vocal command to extend. Maintain the rhythm and the contact on the reins, feeling the horses leaning on your left hand and the leader pull on the traces. It is best that your right hand, which is holding the whip, should not touch your left hand at all as this will give a better feeling and maintain equal tension on all four reins in the left hand. A skilful and subtle hand will adapt to exactly the right amount of tension required in order to extend. After X, ask the leader to return to a steady, forward-going working trot because the one-handed 30-m circle is looming.

6. Halt, rein-back and walk
Rein-back should be taught and then practised at least two or three times in each schooling session. It is most important that you have a very powerful wheeler which has been thoroughly trained.

In the dressage arena you should make a good halt at G, count ten seconds silently without touching your reins which should be completely slack, then call to the leader to back and supplement this command by taking up a quiet tension on the reins. The leader's traces are also slack. It is the backing of the wheeler which produces the tension on the reins and on the traces of the leader who reins himself back automatically.

When the two horses have backed together for four steps, covering about 3 m (10 ft), you must immediately ask them to walk forward.

When backing a tandem, it is essential to halt with the leader, wheeler and carriage exactly in line. If this line is not straight before you begin the manoeuvre, do not back. Practise good halts with every part of the tandem equipage in line.

Finally, walking across the diagonal is a very sad-looking movement. The left hand holds the reins and the right hand has nothing to do except hold the whip at the correct angle. The diagonal seems to go on forever!

7. Transitions of gait or pace and changing reins

Each transition from one pace to another in trot must be done immediately by the leader and wheeler, at exactly the same time and without changing the rhythm. A good quality transition will show natural ease. 'The quality of the pace you take depends on the quality of the last steps of the preceding pace. If the horses go from walk to trot without any modification in their head carriage, it is because the walk had good impulsion' (N. Oliveira).

When the horses go from trot to walk, you 'must call for steadiness with your voice' and send your hand slightly forward while still maintaining contact with their mouths, otherwise the horses will fall on to their forehands in a sloppy manner.

An excellent account of changing the rein has been written by G. Steinbrecht:

To change hand on a circle or a serpentine, you must stop the lateral flexion (bend) of the horse not only by loosening the inside rein but also by taking, at the same time and with more energy, a tension on the outside rein so that, during the change of rein, the help given by the hand will never be stopped, not even for a moment.

Although given by a rider, this advice should be strictly observed by the tandem driver who must keep a constant contact with the horses' mouths and maintain traditional English rein handling throughout the change of direction.

In memoriam N. Oliveira

- 'Impulsion is a moral and physical disposition of the horses to obey as quickly as possible the command to rush forward and, without any help, to maintain their propelling strength. It is the maintenance of power in keeping the rhythm. No impulsion without rhythm; no rhythm without impulsion!'
- 'The horse's impulsion is created by the introduction of the hind legs under the body, which forces the horse to seek the contact of the rider's [driver's] hand, which the hand receives with an "exquisite delicacy".'
- 'When a horse has good impulsion, he is forward going and has no time to create any problems. He is too occupied with his own forward impulsion.'
- 'If the horse has good impulsion, he has muscular energy which flexes well and does not cramp up. He achieves more flexibility when in a good rhythm; he becomes stiffer when he speeds up.'

Amen!

FEI Driving Trials: introduction and dressage

JUDGING SHEET   TEST No. 3 (ADVANCED)

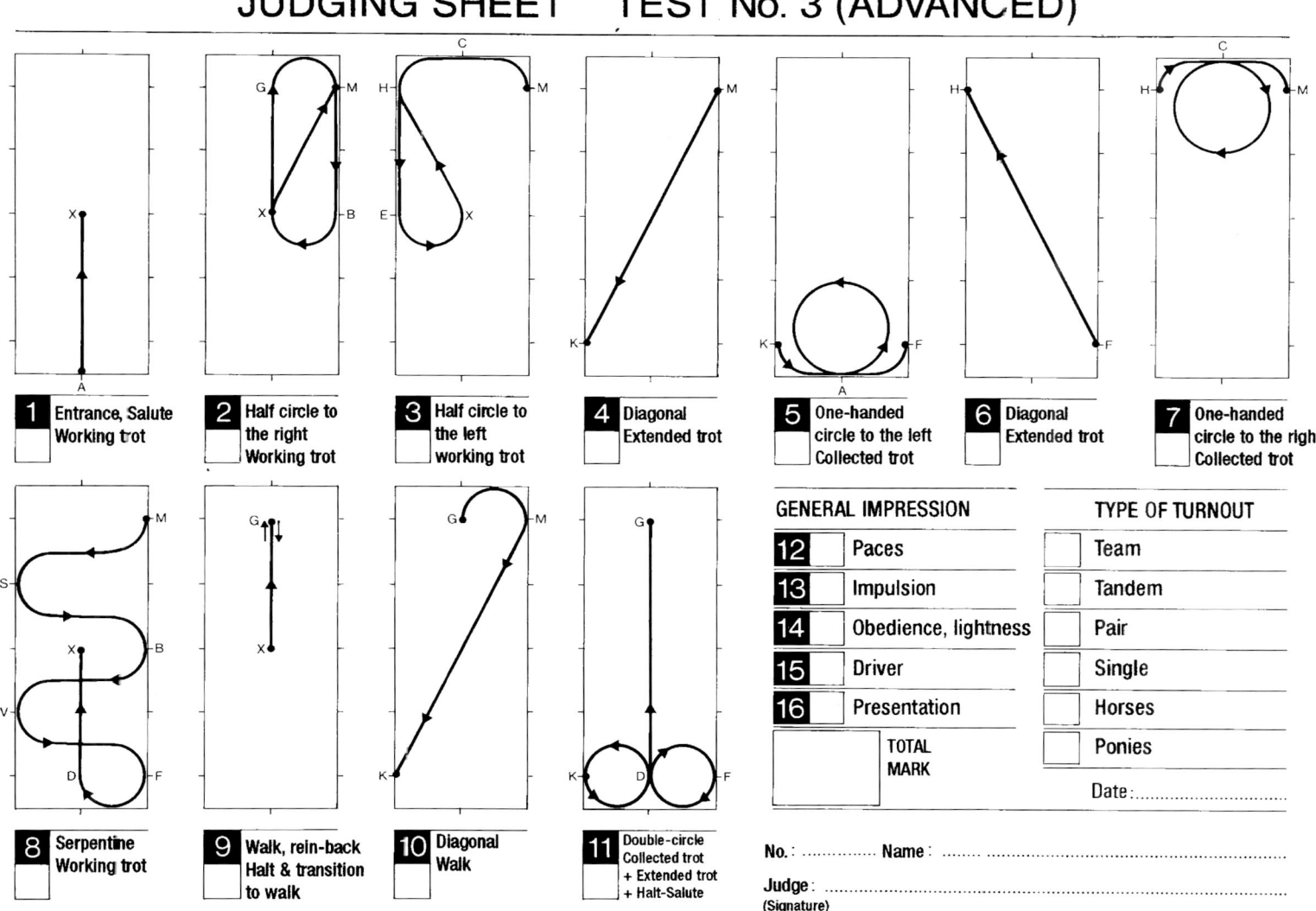

Proposed judge's sheet for Test no. 3.

Rules for tandem dressage competitions

FEI Article 920.5

'The competitor, when driving the Dressage Test, will make the change of movement at the time the leaders reach the point indicated on the test.'

This is fine when changing paces and when halting but it cannot be applied to a tandem whose leader must change direction. It is plain for all to see that if the leader begins to turn at the marker specified in the dressage test, the wheeler and the carriage will cut the corner. It is therefore necessary for the leader to trot a few steps beyond the marker. Only then will the carriage wheels follow the correct track.

The judges

Five judges must sit at C, R, S, V and P. If there are only three judges, they must sit at C, B and E.

The total of the judges' scores will be divided by five or three.

Each judge must judge the tandem equipage on the geometry of the figures, the horses' paces and the line taken by the two wheels of the carriage.

The job of judging is very tiring as it demands constant watchfulness, great concentration and excellent memory in order to recall the marks and observations of previous drivers. A secretary or scribe will help with this duty.

It is helpful if the judge has at his or her disposal the type of sheet which I recommend for each of the three main dressage tests and, for each competitor, a score sheet detailing the allocation of marks, such as the sample sheet I suggest for Test 3.

The marks allocated to 'general impression' deserve careful thought and should not be given hastily in order to snatch time for a quick cup of coffee during the pause between competitors.

These days, tandem driving competitors are becoming more and more skilful and experienced. Each individual point now carries more importance so that the six points given for general impression can make all the difference in the final placing.

'*Errare humanum est*' (to err is human) no longer applies. In modern competitions judges must never make mistakes.

14

FEI Driving Trials: marathon

FEI Competition B

'The object of Competition B – the Marathon – is to test the standard of fitness, stamina, and training of the horses, and the skill, judgment of pace, and horsemanship of the competitor' (FEI 924.1).

The main rules for tandem marathon are the same as for four-in-hand, with only one real exception which concerns the total length of the course. It is divided into three or five sections over a maximum total distance of 27 km (16½ miles). Speed and distance are judged as for a pair.

Rules for tandems, Appendix M (1993)

1. Competitors may take part in International Competitions and Championships for Pony Tandems from the beginning of the year in which they reach the age of 16 ... [and] for Horse Tandems from the beginning of the year they reach their 18th birthday. See General Regulations, Article 124.

The spare horse may only be substituted once. Once a substitution has been made it is irreversible and the horse substituted may not be used again.

Vehicles

2a. A two or four wheeled vehicle suitable for a tandem.
2b. In Competitions A and C there will be no standard outside track width, but the outside track width may not be greater than 160 cm [63 in.].
2c. The vehicle used in Competition B must weigh at least 150 kg [3 cwt] for horses, 90 kg [1¾ cwt] for ponies.
2d. The vehicle must carry:
   In all competitions: one groom
   In Competition B: there will be referees on the carriage or observers on the ground in Sections B, C, D and E.
3. Competitors may enter 4 horses/ponies, but may only bring three for the Event.

The marathon vehicle

This has a platform for the groom at the rear. Since 1993, both two- and four-wheeled vehicles have been allowed at tandem marathons.

The two-wheeled vehicle

Advantages: easy to back and there is less chance of catching a wheel in a marker post.
Disadvantages: not so easy to balance when going up and down hills. There is more danger of turning the vehicle over.

At full speed. Phursac and Okapi, 1987, with the referee on the carriage.

The four-wheeled vehicle

Advantages: greater stability, better braking and the groom is able to balance better.

Disadvantages: if you catch a marker post between a front and back wheel, you may end up being eliminated for exceeding the time limit.

The tandem box seat

A so-called 'tub seat' will keep the driver from falling out. This can be set on the left, right or in the middle as you please.

Two handles should be set on the dashboard to give the driver something to catch hold of if necessary.

The driver must wear *a safety harness*. In dangerous situations the groom can catch hold of this and use it to keep the driver on board. This harness must never be tied to the carriage in case the driver falls out and is dragged.

Nylon harness

A nylon harness is excellent for winter training and tandem driving trials. It is certainly not elegant but it is practical, durable, relatively cheap, comfortable for the animals, unaffected by rain and easy to maintain. Its greatest advantage, however, is that all the harness pieces are very strong and are very unlikely to break. The invention of new materials intended for use in sailing yachts has been of great benefit to horsemen too, producing materials that are of good quality and very convenient to use. In 1993 harness made of polyurethane came on to the market. This material is excellent as it is easy to wash clean of mud.

The bridles

The bridle may be fitted with racing blinkers if you prefer as they improve the angle of vision of the horses. It is most inadvisable to drive without any blinkers at all as this is very dangerous.

The bits

In my opinion, the jointed snaffle bit is the ideal bit for both training and marathon driving. Because of its jointed action, the snaffle is the best bit for steering and is also quite sufficient to stop tandem horses that have been schooled correctly to respond to the hand and voice. Another advantage of the snaffle is that when one is worn by the wheeler, the leader's reins cannot become caught under the bridged cheekpieces of the wheeler's bit. Moreover, it is commonly true that people who use curb bits for driving, which offer three different heights for the adjustment of the reins, still mostly use only the uppermost hole which acts as a snaffle.

When negotiating obstacles in the marathon, the turns may require a very accurate lateral effect to be achieved through the action of the bit and it is true that if the reins are fastened to the bottom or middle bar, they will give very poor lateral action or even none at all. There is also a tendency for the curb chain to be too tight.

Collars

Most drivers use breast collars which necessitate the traces of the wheeler being put to a carriage fitted with a swingle-tree held by a bolt and nut axle. Once, when racing my tandem up a steep hill during a marathon, the bolt, being old and worn, broke. Luckily, the horses continued calmly up the hill in walk while I was forced to jump over the low dashboard and follow them up the track as if long-reining them on foot. Since then, for security, I have preferred to tie the carriage bar with a nylon rope fixed on both sides of each wheel's axle.

I prefer to use a well-fitting full collar on my wheeler. The leader's breast collar can be equipped with traces for tandem bars as well as long English traces.

Tandem bars or long English traces?

Tandem bars Two bars are used: a lead bar and a rear bar. These will assist the driver considerably in the handling of the team in modern competitions.

The lead bar resembles a swingle tree. For a 14-hand team it is about 2 feet 5 inches [74 cm] long with a trace hook at either end. The centre ring goes over a long hook on the middle of the rear bar which is about 1 foot 11 inches [58 cm] long. On each end of this bar is a ring to which 1 foot 9 inches [53 cm] of trace is sewn. There is a spring cock-eye at the end of each short trace which is hooked on to the shaft horse's hame tug buckle. At the centre of the rear bar is a 9-inch [23-cm] chain with a hook at the end which is fastened 'to the kidney link ring or hame chain ring on the shaft horse's hames. A small strap goes from the underneath of the centre of the rear bar through a slot at the end of the centre hook and buckles on a small buckle on the bar. This is put on as a precaution to prevent the lead bar from jumping off.

(S. Walrond, *Encyclopaedia of Carriage Driving*)

Double bars are more frequently used on the continent of Europe. They must be of excellent quality and should not be homemade as this equipment, although specially adapted for getting through the gates of obstacles, does get treated very roughly in difficult situations when it may be struck violently or become hooked up.

Long English traces Even if the leader is wearing a breast collar, it can be equipped with long English traces as well. An elastic strap supports each trace, being attached at one end to a D sewn in the long trace and, at the other, to the wheeler's breast collar. This strap is especially useful when turning a corner in walk.

Safety measures in marathon tandem driving

- Duplicate the leader's traces with a nylon cord if they are made out of leather.
- Duplicate the attachment of the swingle tree to the leader traces and, even more important, the attachment of the hind bar to the breast collar.
- Protect the horses' legs.
- You should be aware that the spare equipment required by the rules in a competition is insufficient for a genuine repair and that you should also carry wire, pliers, strong string, adhesive tape and a sharp Swiss Army knife.
- Carry two halters and detachable tethers.
- A spare whip is not only compulsory but indispensable. Place it in the carriage so that you can put your hand on it immediately in an emergency.

The rules of the course (1993)

The course is divided into five sections, each of which is driven over a maximum distance at designated gaits and maximum speeds as outlined in the table.

Time and distance in the marathon (FEI)

	Max. distance	Min. distance	Pace	Speeds Horses	Ponies
Section A	10 km		Free	15 kph	14 kph
Section B	1200 m	800 m	Walk	7 kph	6 kph
Section C	5 km		Trot	19 kph	17 kph
Section D	1200 m	800 m	Walk	7 kph	6 kph
Section E	10 km		Trot	15 kph	14 kph

- Each section is delimited by signposts for 'Start' and 'Finish'.

- Sections B and D are driven in walk over rather flat, minor roads.
- The entire route is marked by yellow arrows.
- Red and white boundary flags or indicators are used to mark both sides of compulsory sections of the course and to indicate changes of direction. The red flag must always be on the competitor's right-hand side; white on the left.
- These red and white flags will be numbered consecutively and must be clearly visible. Compulsory sections may be placed anywhere on the course, regardless of obstacle zones, forest, roads, hills and slopes, old bridges, small streams, etc.
- Section E is the obstacles section. They can be natural or manmade. Each obstacle is roped off from the public for safety reasons. The number of obstacles is strictly limited to eight.

Sections A, B, C and D

- In Section A, any pace may be taken. This offers no particular difficulties for a tandem but you must keep up a constant speed to cover the first 9 km ($5\frac{1}{2}$ miles) in good time. The speed of the last kilometre can then be adjusted to make sure you cross the finishing line at exactly the right speed of 15 kph (9.3 mph) for horses and 14 kph (8.7 mph) for a pony tandem.
- In Section B the walk must not be neglected. You must seek to achieve a regular and lively walk with the leader's traces constantly lightly taut so that the equipage is straight as it passes the end of section marker.
- In Section C the trot should be faster than 20 kph for horses and 19 kph for ponies because you must take into account the various hills, crossings and places where you need to slow down. If you catch up with another competitor, you should not hesitate to overtake after warning the other driver courteously of your intention.
- Section D. This walking section is necessary to allow the horses' pulse rate to drop to normal before the veterinary surgeons make their statutory examination at the end of the section. It is necessary to maintain a regular rhythm in the walk, especially from the leader who will then allow the wheeler to work less hard and so calm its heart beat.

Section E – the obstacles zone

- Each obstacle is sectioned off by a line of flags and ropes which have been inspected by the FEI Technical Delegate (TD). There will be one or more compulsory openings or gates.
- The course itself is barred to spectators for reasons of safety.
- The 'penalty zone' is clearly defined in FEI rules, 6th edition (1993).

> Surrounding the obstacle there is a penalty zone measured 20 m from the nearest flags defining the obstacle, except where natural or man-made features interfere and the Technical Delegate grants an exception... Entrances and exits to the penalty zones are defined with un-numbered compulsory red and white flags. Any barrier for crowd restraint must be at least 1 m beyond the penalty zone. Once any part of the team or vehicle has entered the penalty zone, competitors are liable to penalties as defined in Article 927.

It is not permitted to enter any part of an obstacle before first passing through the compulsory red and white starting flags for the obstacle in question. Contravening this article means elimination. (FEI)

Artificial obstacles

Definition
- The maximum number of obstacles, natural or artificial, in Section E is eight; the minimum is five and championship courses must have at least seven.
- The obstacles must be at least 200 m (219 yd) apart and the last obstacle must not be less than 500 m (547 yd) from the finish unless the TD grants an exception.
- Obstacles consist of elements (posts, water, trees, banks) with one or more compulsory openings – 'the gates'. Obstacles may be constructed where there are no natural elements or to modify natural features.
- Obstacle gates are defined by pairs of red and white markers or flags.
- Gates which may be driven in any order have no letter, while gates to be driven in a prescribed order are marked A, B, C, D, E, F.
- No obstacle gate may be narrower than 2.5 m (8 ft) and at least one route to each gate should be no narrower than 2.5 m.
- The gates must be at least 1.3 m ($4\frac{1}{4}$ ft) high. No element inside the gate may be lower than 1.3 m.

Dislodgeable elements Obstacles with dislodgeable elements have been compulsory for all international events since 1993.

Gates have been the source of many accidents for

A nasty obstacle on the marathon course.

carriages, horses, grooms and drivers, and the use of dislodgeable elements seems a very good innovation from the authors of the 1993 rules, who accepted two styles: a dislodgeable post or a dislodgeable rod or stick attached to the post with Velcro.

6. ... It is obligatory to have double the number of dislodgeable elements as obstacles. No obstacle may have more than three dislodgeable elements. Two penalty points are incurred per element knocked down ... The displacement of a dislodgeable element must always be penalised whenever it occurs. A driver or a groom preventing a dislodgeable element from falling is

FEI Driving Trials: marathon

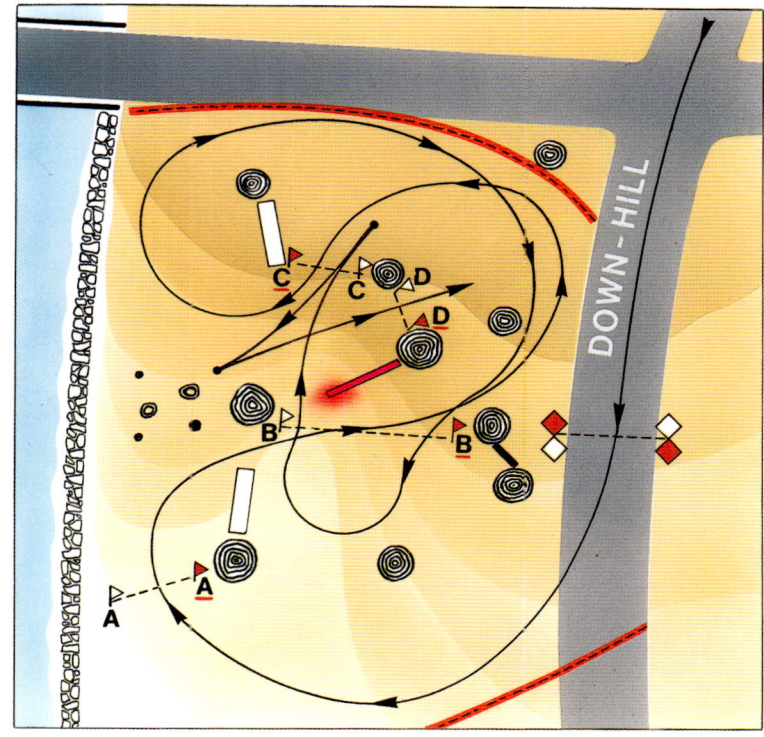

Gates already cleared: the drawing shows the tandem hugging the stone-wall to the left and turning right before running straight through the gate. (M. Berthélémy)

penalised with ten penalty points.
7. ... Competitors are authorised to use any pace in the penalty zone. (FEI Article 925)

- The obstacle judge notes the time between entry to and exit from the obstacle.

- Competitors must go through each lettered element of an obstacle in the correct sequence – A, B, C, D ... If the driver makes an error, he or she incurs 20 penalty points for each error corrected and elimination if the error is not corrected.
- Time and penalty points make the winners and the losers. The most important thing is to keep an eye on the chronometer but the most disagreeable thing is to rush and get yourself jammed in an obstacle as a result.
- No obstacle that necessitates a rein-back is permitted, but it may be performed through an obstacle already cleared.

Natural obstacles

Depending on the imagination of the course builder, these may be many and varied but they may not be preposterous or dangerous. Posts, walls, trees, houses and old barns are all available but two sorts of natural obstacle feature most often – ups and downs, which can appear terrifying, and water obstacles.

Hills Hills are always dangerous if you wish to follow an oblique line or have to make a turn as you are going up or down, which is when the risk of turning the vehicle over is greatest. When going uphill, the leader must work at full traces but if the leader is then asked to turn, the wheeler is apt to be thrown over, so beware! Going downhill is especially dangerous in a two-wheeled vehicle if you do not shorten all four reins quite considerably and very quickly. In contrast, backing down in a two-wheeled carriage is very easy and can possibly be the better choice.

To ford or not to ford? England, 1861. (Achenbach *magazine, Switzerland*)

Water Fording a small, muddy stream can be very alarming if a rotten branch is lying completely hidden in the mud. This happened to me while I was galloping my tandem team through water during winter training. We were having great fun until I was suddenly thrown out of the right-hand side of the carriage and dragged for about 20 m through the mud while holding on to my buckled reins. Just as I was about to make contact with the right wheel of the carriage, my well-disciplined team came to a halt and disaster was averted. We still reminisce about that particular adventure on long winter evenings in front of the fire because it so happened that, on that day, my groom was none other than my charming wife! The moral of this story is that you must always be very careful with water obstacles and go through them on foot during your inspection of the course.

Prince Philip tells the following story from his own experience:

> A sort of woodland pond also featured in, I think it was, Section E of the Sopot course. On the reconnaissance of the course all the competitors were stopped at this pond to watch a demonstration by a pair of horses being driven through it. In spite of the fact that the cart had pneumatic tyres I noticed that at one point it fairly leapt into the air, nearly spilling the driver. Everyone seemed to be quite satisfied about the depth but I was a bit suspicious about the bumps and later on I came back to the scene on my own, or almost on my own as I was being followed by a carload of police. I am not quite sure what went through their minds as they saw me taking off first my shoes and socks and then my trousers before wading into the pond clad in a shirt. It didn't take me long to find the cause of the bump: there were two very large rocks lying on the otherwise sandy bottom. A word with the course designer settled the problem promptly and two rocks about the size of the Stone of Scone probably still repose gracefully at the water's edge.
>
> (*Competition Carriage Driving*)

Winter and spring tandem training

To cover about 27.5 km (17 miles) at a quick trot and two active walks while passing through eight obstacles is a great physical strain on the horses of the tandem team, especially the wheeler, and it is quite obvious that thorough preparation in the right conditions will give the horses the best chance of success. A well-thought-out training programme for horses, driver and groom will give everyone the mental and physical stamina that is necessary when one is permanently struggling against time.

Training the horses in winter is easy if you are able to work through your training schedule regularly and quietly on good roads in suitable weather and without running the risk of both you and your horses being killed by heavy lorries! It is also a good idea to ride your tandem horses for a few weeks in an indoor school as this is an excellent way to promote good health, strong muscles and an equable temperament.

The two horses (and your third or substitute) must be ridden and driven singly at least twice a week during February and March. You should practise going through single obstacles. When work is over, you should return the horses to the comfort of their boxes and offer good quality hay, food, vitamins and your thanks for work well done.

Training through water obstacles

You must seek out or build a very easy and safe water obstacle. At first, you should lead the horse in on foot and then ride it, stopping in the water and then going forward, turning round, backing, going on and then recrossing from the other direction. Next, you must drive the horse singly, doing the same things and stopping in the water to let the horse drink . The training pool or stream must obviously be at least 10 m (33 ft) across to prevent the horse from remaining too close to the edge. There are some otherwise excellent horses that absolutely refuse to follow a stream or cross a ford. Once you begin to shout at them, it is guaranteed that they will never change their minds.

Only when your two tandem horses and the spare horse have all learned the water lesson well and have sufficient individual knowledge of what you require of them should you harness the two horses in line to the carriage and drive through the water as often as possible.

Pulling

Everyone knows that the wheeler is the only horse pulling when you are driving easily along a flat road but you must teach the leader to pull as well and for this purpose you must find a suitable hilly track. The steeper the hill, the better the leader will learn to do his share of the work.

Drive slowly up the slope at an energetic walk or possibly in trot and stop when halfway up, keeping the traces in tension, then start again, calling to the leader first.

Obstacles

You must build an obstacle course for training over and you should change the style of some of the obstacles every two or three weeks so that your horses do not get so bored with the same old promenade that they become blasé. The one thing you must never do is to ask your horses to stop in the middle of an obstacle in order to take a good look at it. And don't forget to carry some nice titbit in your pocket!

Approaching the obstacle

The minimum width of the gate between the two markers

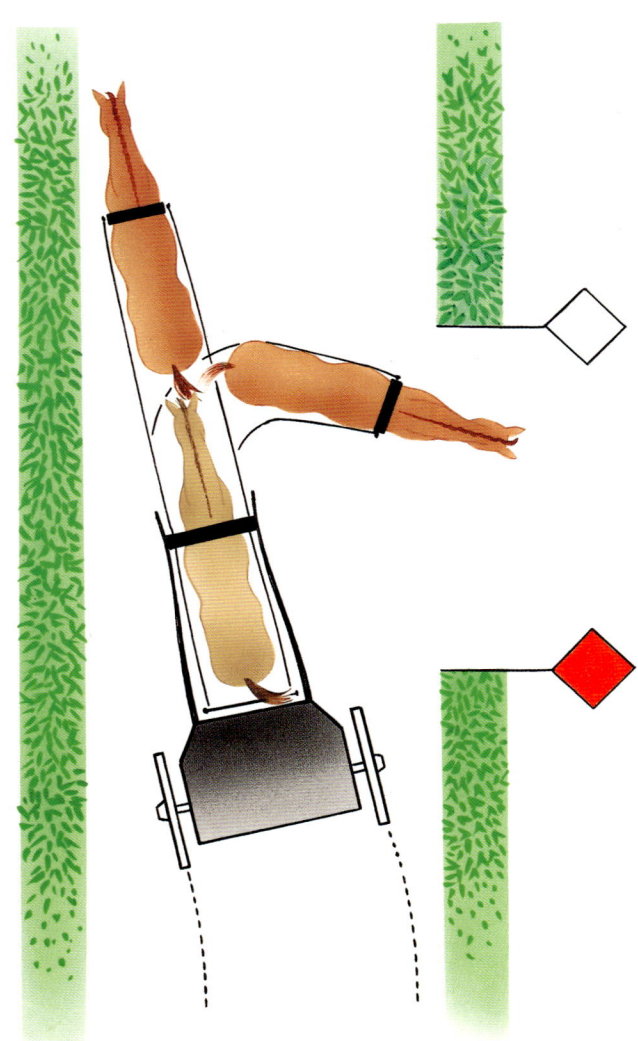

A rather tricky entrance. (M. Berthélémy)

must be 2.5 m (just over 8 ft) and the approach to it should be no less than 2.5 m wide. This presents no difficulty when you are driving the tandem team straight forward in your approach but things become rather more difficult if you come in obliquely to the gate or at a right angle or even an acute angle.

As you can see on the drawing below, in order to turn right, you must wait until the leader reaches the extreme left marker, at which point you must stop the wheeler but encourage the leader to continue in walk to the right until the horses articulate as necessary. Only then should the wheeler begin to move again and you can negotiate the gate without allowing the right wheel to touch the red marker. This manoeuvre is perhaps easier with a four-wheeled vehicle ... provided you don't have to back your team.

The sequence of the A, B, C, D, E sections

To maintain the tempo of a good working or quick trot through the gates, or even to flash through at full gallop, is the sign of a very good driver but do not forget that it is compulsory to return to a quick trot before exiting from the obstacle, i.e. before the leader's nose goes out of the gate.

A final word

You will find great satisfaction in training your tandem team. As time goes by you will discover that you get on better and better with your horses and that mistakes and accidents are reduced to a minimum. Bring all the enthusiasm you have to your training sessions and they will become fun both for you and your horses.

Walking the course

In most equestrian competitions it is regular practice for both officials and competitors to inspect the course before riding or driving over it.

About 48 hours before the marathon competition begins, the course is inspected by the course designer or official Technical Delegate, who together have been responsible for laying out and marking the course, building the obstacles and measuring the route. All the competitors and their grooms follow along behind the official party. Every obstacle is studied keenly and you may find that you need to return to some of them many times to work out exactly how to drive through each one. Some obstacles are very tricky and could be driven in three or four different ways but my advice is that once you have made your decision, do not try to change it at the last minute because you will have no time to think once you are engaged in negotiating the obstacle.

Your groom will help you to follow the route exactly as the two of you agreed to do when you walked the course earlier. Trying to find the happy medium between making good time and being reckless can be quite difficult, especially when some of the obstacles turn out to be brain teasers!

The most important aspect of the tandem equipage is its length. You must be aware of the exact distance from the nose of the wheeler to the axle of the carriage and also the exact width of the axle itself.

A tandem is a vulnerable equipage and audacity will

Official inspection of the marathon course, according to Jacquot, the talented humourist, painter and rider. (L'Eperon, illustrated supplement, in memory of the late Prince Ali Khan)

Style and speed through a marathon obstacle. D. Würgler, 1992.

not always pay, no matter how good a driver you are. Often it is better to choose a long route without any chance of a stop than to go for a shorter one and risk your vehicle getting stuck in the obstacle. Your groom has the job of navigator. He or she also regulates the speed of the tandem and must keep an eye on the time between the entry to and exit from each obstacle. A good tandem will go through an obstacle in round about 30 seconds, which gives four to five minutes for all eight obstacles – the theoretical time of Section E.

Fixed obstacles

You must remember that a tandem equipage is put to a rather fragile vehicle, even when made of modern materials. Consequently, there are some people who believe that a tandem team is not suitable for marathon driving. Despite this, you will see wonderful tandem drivers, handling their buckled reins expertly at a fine speed and who are even able to get their horses to change legs at exactly the same time when cantering through the gateway into an obstacle. However, you may also see disagreeable things, such as the trapping of a wheel in a fixed marker, and this is why it seems logical that all artificial obstacles should have dislodgeable markers in tandem marathons. None the less, until there is an official international ruling about this in the building of gates, we must continue to drive through some few fixed obstacles.

15
FEI Driving Trials: obstacles

FEI Competition C

The object of Competition C is to test the fitness, obedience and suppleness of the horses after the Marathon and skill and competence of the competitor.

(FEI Article 931)

The fitness of the tandem horses or ponies following the marathon depends on the anatomical and physiological state of the animals after a great effort, sometimes in adverse weather conditions. Excess heat is worse than cold; not so long ago driven horses died of dehydration caused by prolonged effort in humid weather.

Timing through the cones, Hamburg 1992.

Track width and distance between obstacles (FEI 1993)

TANDEMS	Gap between two cones: cm wider than track width	Max. track width	Distance between individual obstacles (max.)	L Double L m	U Box m	Serpentine m	Zig-Zag m	Speed m/min.
Horses	60/max. 30/min.	160	15 m	4/4	4/5	12	12	200/220
Ponies	60/max. 30/min.	160	12 m	3/3 (entry & exit)	3/4	10	10	220/230

The principles of Competition C

The basic principle is to drive the two horses in tandem between pairs of plastic cones, 30 cm (1 ft) high, set out over a circuit that has been made as difficult as possible. The course is covered at a quick trot or even canter or full gallop over the long, straight sections. The carriage must be the two-wheeled type already used in the dressage. There is no standard track width, as in the dressage test, but the outside width may not exceed 160 cm (63 in.) for horses and 140 cm (55 in.) for ponies, which reduces the boring business of measuring and changing the width between the cones all the time.

A plastic ball sits in a slight depression on the top of each cone and this will fall off if the cone is struck. If either one or both balls falls, there is a penalty of 5 points.

The minimum width between a pair of cones is 190 cm (75 in.).

• Only three multiple obstacles may be incorporated by the organisers. These do, however, make the course much more fun. Show jumping poles can be used at a height of between 40 and 60 cm (16–24 in.). It is also possible to build L-shaped obstacles, double Ls, Us or boxes with three elements at right angles, marked A, B and C. Knocking down one pole costs 5 points, two bars cost 10 points and three bars cost 15 points.

• Water obstacles should be 3 m (10 ft) wide with sloping sides. The water should be 20–40 cm (8–16 in.) deep and there should be cones with dislodgeable markers at the entrance and exit. The cones should be marked A and B and should be set 2.5 m (8 ft) apart.

• There can be a wooden bridge with different entrances and cones marked A and B at the entrance and exit.

• A serpentine can be made of no more than four posts set in a straight line. The posts should be 12 m (39 ft) apart for tandem horses and 10 m (33 ft) apart for ponies, with four dislodgeable markers set on alternate sides and marked A, B, C and D.

• A zig-zag consists of four pairs of cones set 12 m (39 ft) apart for both horses and ponies, with alternate left and right cones set in a straight line.

• Cones and balls are also set inside the multiple obstacles and at the entrance to and the final exit from the course.

The circuit

The route is laid out over a fairly flat area measuring 70 ×120 m (230 × 394 yd) and the length of the course when driven will be between 500 and 800 m (1,640–2,625 yd), which will be measured exactly in order to calculate the theoretical time of the course.

The course will contain seventeen cone obstacles and three multiple obstacles set at random intervals. The tandem team must be driven through all of the obstacles. The course may contain no more than twenty obstacles in total and they must be set at over 15 m (49 ft) apart for horse tandems and 12 m (39 ft) apart for pony tandems.

On the course, the obstacles are indicated by a pair of panels, coloured red on the right and white on the left of the obstacle. These panels are numbered from one to twenty. The design of the circuit depends on the flair and imagination of the course designer and its level of difficulty will test the skill and fighting spirit of each competitor. The ability to negotiate obstacles at speed will be necessary.

A good tandem course builder will create a very open course for this unique form of driving, with long stretches without obstacles leading from one part of the field to another in order to show off the elegant style of the turnouts.

Time

The time allowed is based on a speed of 200 metres per minute (219 yd per min.) for horses and 220 mpm (240 yd min.) for ponies. If the official time is exceeded, penalty points are awarded at the rate of 0.5 for every second or part of a second over the maximum.

Only a driver who is well prepared and has trained his or her horses thoroughly will achieve the optimum time. Drivers may drive two-handed if they wish.

Training

It is virtually impossible to train at home for Competition C if you have no cones to set out as obstacles over routes of varying difficulty.

T. Velstra schools his tandem horses through the cones first. He likes to pile six cones up, one on top of the other, and thus create two tall markers which look like the entrance to a gate. This greatly impresses the leader and wheeler, who are afraid of knocking them down.

Each day the cones will be placed closer and closer until they are 1.8 m (6 ft) apart. Each day, one cone will be removed. The tandem team is asked to drive faster and faster in a straight line through the cones.

I find it easier to begin this training in a schooling arena where the boundaries of 100 × 40 m (109 × 44 ft) are already well known to the horses. Once the team is used to passing straight through the cones, I begin to drive through the two cones at a slightly oblique angle and almost allow the wheeler to follow the leader at his own discretion. When it seems possible, I ask for greater speed.

When the team becomes more reliable and begins to show a natural respect for the cones and when the leader begins to aim spontaneously for the mid point between the two cones, then you can strap a chronometer to your wrist and begin to compete against yourself. The wheeler must be told to go on because this is the horse with the harder work to do as the leader will not tighten its traces fully. Nowadays, many drivers like to carry a modern whip with a long stick and shorter thong which they can crack. This is certainly the best way in which to encourage the team and push it instantly into canter. However, the 'tact' that I mention below (chap. 17) must always be regarded as the driver's greatest aid to impulsion and precision.

Competition driving

Just as with the marathon, the course is walked with the course designer one hour before the start. Only the driver is allowed to walk the course. You must do this in the correct order and should try to memorise it exactly so that you are in no doubt about the route you will follow.

Cone obstacles

In order to drive a direct line to bring the horses in at right angles to the obstacle, it is necessary to get the horses on to a straight line in good time before reaching the cones. This means that the long tandem equipage must be handled very quickly immediately after obstacle 1 if you wish to meet obstacle 2 correctly with leader, wheeler and carriage exactly in line. If you meet each obstacle correctly, you will be in the best position to aim for the next one. A slightly oblique line is possible and can save time but it is much riskier and must be practised thoroughly.

Multiple obstacles

U-shaped and box obstacles are the most difficult because both require a 180-degree turn which necessitates keeping the leader out on the outer border for as long as possible. Neither the leader nor the carriage must be allowed to touch the cone that is sometimes placed on the inner border by the course designer. On one occasion I allowed my leader to go too far and then watched him jump over the bar he found in front of him. He did this very correctly, without touching it, and remained absolutely in line but, alas, we were unable to follow him!

The bridge

First of all, the leader must be willing to go up on to the bridge. If you feel the horse hesitating from a distance, you must urge it on in a straight line at a balanced, energetic trot with the reins gently tightened. Then, if you feel the horse hesitate, you will be in a position to use the reins to straighten it up and also to push the wheeler forward while shouting out the name of the leader. If you are skilful enough, this is just the right time to show how well you can crack your whip. Once on the bridge, the leader should continue without problems.

The water obstacle

If your leader usually makes faces in front of water, don't struggle too long here. If the horse will not go in, ask your groom to get down and go to the horse's head to lead it across the ford. A penalty of 5 points and wet feet are better than time elimination.

The serpentine and zig-zag

These are great fun for both the driver and the horses. Maintain a quick tempo which is better than trying to cut the corners and risking touching a cone or, even worse, the marker.

Beating the clock

This is the most testing obstacle of all. For tandem horses 200 m per minute (219 yd/min.) demands a speed of 12 kph (7½ mph), which is very fast indeed if the course is difficult and the turns are tight. In order to make the time, you will have to keep the horses trotting on energetically at a good tempo, or even galloping, which is not fgorbidden.

The last word

> The ingenuity of the designer of an obstacle driving course is somewhat restricted by the precise rules which circumscribe it, but he can position his obstacles and cones so as to form courses which will vary between being virtually impossible to drive at the required speed and being able to be driven easily at a speed of 50 m per minute [55 yd/min.] faster than required.
>
> (T. Coombs)

The good tandem course builder will choose the second option.

At the end of Competition C, the placing of the tandem drivers should not depend entirely on their speed because this is not the sole object of tandem driving, which should be rewarded more for the driver's skill and technique.

A final word on marathon and obstacle driving

- Do not forget about the time penalties and be aware of your time.
- Do not take foolish risks with obstacles and incur penalties needlessly.
- Do not get yourself eliminated by mistake! This is done by:
 – disconnecting and leading the leader through any part of the obstacle during the marathon;
 – any error of course before passing the exit flag.

> Competition C may be conducted either on the basis of the number of obstacles knocked over which will be known as the Fault Competition, or against the clock which will be known as the Time Competition.
>
> The Fault Competition will be used for Combined Driving Events.

Fault competition

Each competitor will be timed by a stop-watch or an electronic timing device from the moment the nose of the leader crosses the start and finish lines. The time allowed is worked out on the basis of a speed of 200 mpm (219 yd/min.) for horses and 220 mpm (240 yd/min.) for ponies for a first round, and 220 mpm for horses and 230 mpm (251 yd/min.) for ponies in a drive-off.

Time competition

Tandems are rarely asked to compete in time competitions but when they do so the number, type and dimensions of the obstacles, the length of the course and the running of the competition will be the same as for a fault competition.
- When penalties are assessed, penalty seconds will be

substituted for faults.
• The winner will be the driver to complete the course with the lowest number of penalty seconds.

Three-day events
To discover the overall winner, the result sheets of competitions A (dressage), B (marathon) and C (obstacle driving) are combined and this establishes the ranking of the drivers.
• The driver with the fewest penalty points over all three sections is the winner.
• If there is a draw for a placing, the winner will be the driver who amassed fewer penalty points in the marathon.
• If there is still a draw, the driver who performed the better dressage test will be the winner.
• If first place is drawn, the winner will be decided by a drive-off.

'When you told me about your tandem, I imagined something different!' (Joyeux, Swiss Tandem Club, 1990)

16

Tandem showing and other competitions

The turnout of a tandem for showing

The equipage
Equipage is a French word meaning an elegant carriage drawn by well-bred horses and driven by a master and carrying the master's invited guests and grooms. This term is invariably used in Britain when talking about tandem and four-in-hand driving. The turnout described below is suitable both for showing and for dressage.

The British tandem driver or whip
The tandem driver is also referred to as 'a whip'. A gentleman driver should wear a black or grey top hat, a black or grey coat, a white shirt with stiff collar and a grey neck tie, grey trousers, grey socks and black, polished shoes. A carnation in the left-hand buttonhole is fashionable but not compulsory.

A whip who prefers a more sporting look will make an equally good impression on the judges by wearing a black or grey bowler hat, but certainly not a chestnut-brown one, which is sometimes worn by a groom.

The driver's apron
I do not care for the modern type of apron that is now seen at nearly every competition, both in Britain and internationally. This is made of a material that is too light and is bound with a gaily coloured braid that is identical to the travelling rug of the owner's horses and has his or her initials in one corner. This apron is worn so long that it covers up the driver's shoes, which makes mounting and dismounting from a tandem carriage difficult. Whatever became of discreet elegance?

In Britain two types of rug are traditionally worn.
- The knee apron covers the knees, reaching from the waist to half-way down the legs. The lower part of the trousers and the shoes are visible. This apron is made of fairly heavy, plain woollen cloth or another good quality material.
- The light rug is even smaller. It is not actually an apron at all but merely a square of cotton or linen or a carefully folded travelling rug, often of Tattersal check, which covers only the thighs and is simply tucked in under the hips.

The English whip
The driver carries a blackthorn tandem whip (rather than a fibreglass one) in his or her right hand. The driver's grip should cover the upper silver collar of the handle in order to balance the whip properly. The right hand rests on the reins in front of the left hand.

The whip must be held at an angle of about 40 degrees to the left and about 40 degrees upwards, with its double

Sue and Bill Vine showing their tandem team, Domino and Marco, put to an English tandem club cart. Smith's Lawn, Windsor, 1977.

thong hanging correctly with no kinks in it.

The most singular tandem whip that I have ever seen had a very unusual stick. It comprised a very, very small tandem horn, the minute trumpet of which formed part of the base of the whip, while, towards the upper part of the handpiece, above the collar, the mouth of the horn projected obliquely in the same direction as the whip. I asked the owner to play this instrument for me, which to my eyes did not seem a properly useful object nor, to my ears, in perfect harmony! As all tandem drivers are aware, blowing a tandem horn is a difficult enterprise at the best of times.

The lady driver

Everything said above about the apron and whip is applicable to ladies. The lady's clothing is not as formal as that of a gentleman, however. The hat should be a small grey, black or beige bowler or any other type of felt hat but its brim must be narrow. A smart suit or longish dress and nice, low-heeled, light-coloured shoes are always suitable. It seems appropriate to remind the reader at this point of the 'seven ages of woman': (1) baby; (2) child; (3) girl; (4) young lady; (5) young lady; (6) young lady; (7) young lady!

To complete the driver's appearance, it is important not to forget his or her seat on the box, and the correct holding of the whip and the gloves, which are mentioned on the checklist.

The tandem groom

> Groom's livery ... was not modified after the turn of the last century, and should not be altered from its original form. Top boots must be worn, without garter straps, and the tops may be brown or almost white 'champagne' ones ... The white breeches may be slightly cream coloured but should, ideally, not be very lightweight nylon ones ...
>
> The livery coat should hang to the mid-way point of the wearer's thigh. It may be black or of any essential dark whole colour to complement the colours of the carriage. There should be six buttons down the front of the coat extending to the wearer's waist, but five only are permissible for very short grooms. There should be three pairs of buttons evenly spaced from the waist to the bottom of the coat down the skirts at the back of it. Buttons should be brass if the harness is brass mounted or silver if the harness mountings are white metal ...
>
> A stiffly starched stand-up collar, without the wings which are appropriate with evening dress, should have a made-up 'Newmarket tie' fastened round it and the two folds of this should be fastened to the flap behind them with a small round-headed stick-pin ...
>
> Liveried carriage grooms must wear black top hats ... Cockades are by no means obligatory.
>
> (T. Coombs, *Horse Driving Trials*)

However, the male groom is not always very happy with his statutory black top hat rammed down on his head, his white tie, black livery, white breeches, black boots – and black thoughts to match.

During showing or presentation he should preferably stand in front of the leader. He should not hold the horse unless this becomes necessary and then never by the reins. He must stand up straight and look the leader in the eye.

When the team is moving on, the groom in a tandem gig may look almost cheerful but he must not speak during a dressage test, otherwise the driver may be eliminated. In a dog cart or tandem cart, the groom must remain sitting and be perfectly still in order not to upset the balance of the two-wheeled carriage unless he is required to move when driving up or downhill.

In the early hours of the morning at the beginning of the driving season, the tandem groom must remain imperturbable during the seemingly endless show presentation even although he may be freezing without a rug, which is reserved strictly for the driver and passenger. Alternatively, he may be close to expiring in the heat of mid-August when his black coat absorbs the sun's rays. Indeed, the tandem groom's lot is not a happy one!

The old, established rules governing the behaviour and duties of a four-in-hand groom are rigid and fixed but they are not quite so strict for a tandem groom. If the driver dresses in a sporting style and does not wear a top hat, the groom may wear stable dress: 'Correct stable dress for a man consists ideally of black polished shoes or ankle boots, a pair of grey day trousers and a grey or pepper and salt tweed jacket, a white stiff collar and black or soberly patterned tie, a black bowler hat and brown leather gloves'.

(T. Coombs)

The girl groom A girl groom will look less austere than a man in a low black top hat. If the tandem driver wears a bowler, however, his girl groom may also wear a black bowler or even a hunting cap and stock. She may wear white breeches and boots or even light-coloured jodhpurs with black jodhpur boots. Jumpers, bright modern blouses and jeans should all be strictly avoided!

No groom at all In a tandem equipage, a lady or gentleman seated beside the driver does not have to dress as a groom. Likewise, in a four-seater, two-wheeled carriage, it is also possible to have no groom seated on the rear bench and to carry one to three passengers.

When a tandem without a groom enters the showing arena, no one will dismount to stand at the leader's head, thus demonstrating the exemplary behaviour of this horse. If a passenger were to dismount to act as a groom, a very fussy judge would be displeased.

FEI Presentation

A sample checklist is shown which can be used as a thorough self-check for tandem presentation. Under FEI regulations, there is a maximum total of 50 points for general impression.

The appearance of the driver and grooms, the cleanliness, fit, match and condition of the harness, horses, and vehicle will be judged.

(FEI Article 920, 1993)

Presentation will be judged by the Ground Jury as an item of the General Impression, marked while the Dressage Test is being driven.

(FEI Article 921, 1993)

British showing classes

Showing classes are held at numerous horse shows during the summer months. Sallie Walrond, Chairman of the Tandem Club of Great Britain, organises annual meets at many venues throughout the British Isles, at which new members to the club are encouraged.

The same checklist as for FEI presentation can be used for the judging of the tandem equipage at halt.

A drive of about four to ten miles (6.5–16 km) is sometimes held as part of the private driving class. Turnouts are sent out along a pre-arranged route after the preliminary judging. The judge is driven round the course in a motor car and he stops at intervals to watch the class as it drives past. Speed is not taken into account but the way of going is scrutinised: a straight-moving leader who covers plenty of ground with each stride will be more desirable than one of showy action who makes little progress and a lot of fuss. A tandem team whose horses are traffic-shy, excitable or excessive pullers are not ideal. The competitors then return to the ring for final judging.

The BDS Windsor Horse Show, 1993

Every year many beautiful tandems come to the Windsor Show.

> The official BDS meet will be held with the drive through Windsor Home Park and Concours d'Elégance for the Janet Johnstone Memorial Trophy. It is open to BDS members only and vehicles must be of traditional type, i.e. *a vehicle of traditional profile and identifiable type to resemble the design of a carriage builder before early 20th century.* The vehicle may be made from modern materials but must have traditional springing and carry lamps. Whips must of course be carried, passengers as well as drivers must wear hats and gloves and use knee rugs. These conditions must be strictly adhered to.
>
> (BDS *Newsletter* N° 173)

Different types of tandem

A pony tandem equipage

These days more and more well-trained, smart pony tandems are to be seen at shows and trials. The main difficulty in the presentation of a pony tandem is in finding a team that shows harmony of size between 10 and 14 hh. There is also the problem that old carriages for ponies are becoming very rare and more and more sought after,

Checklist for a tandem presentation

Horses	Breeding, match, health, cleanliness, mane and tail, foot, shoes.
Harness of both	Identical bridles, adjustment of blinkers, throatlatch, noseband. Wheeler has bar bit, leader often does not Collars or breast collar (sometimes leader has breast collar, wheeler has full collar), with false martingale.
Harness of the wheeler	Bridle with terrets, Roger rings or bearing rein swivel. Hame tugs with an eye. Large saddle with two roller bar terrets. Quality of regular breeching: false, full or long. Traces.
Harness of the leader	Simple bridle. Narrow saddle with leather loops or keepers for traces. A pad from a pair harness is acceptable. Long traces or tandem-bars (if any).
Reins	English reins.
Leathers	Colour, condition, security of all the billets (buckled straps).
Carriage	Type, age, cleanliness, paint condition, shafts, tyres or wheel irons, whip socket, seat cushions, hood. Spare case. Tool kit.
Driver	Attitude on the box seat. Gloves. Whip, thong, furling and holding. Groom or passenger. Appointments: aprons, liveries, umbrella, tandem horn and case.
Final overall impression	Style, colour, and harmony.

while replicas become more and more expensive, although many of the modern pony carriages are built to a very high standard.

A hunting tandem

There is an old English tradition of going to a meet in a tandem turnout with the leader already saddled. The driver should wear either pink or a black jacket, as should the passengers of the dog cart. The tandem groom, however, should be dressed as usual. I can recall the type of heavy tandem carriage called a 'going to cover cart' which was used for transporting terriers, pickaxes and shovels for digging out the earth if the fox went to ground. Today, such hunting tandems are usually only seen at international meetings and hunting or agricultural shows in Britain.

An English friend of mine, who has taken part in many tandem shows, describes the preparation of his turnout in the following way:

> First of all, there must be a perfect display by my two harnessed horses, my carriage, myself and my groom. I take pains over my posture on the box, wishing to appear friendly and imposing yet not conceited. Finally, I wish to create an air of things well done: in the cleanliness and grooming of both horses and the perfect maintenance of the harness which should always look like new with shining brass, fresh paintwork and clean lamps. I am concerned not to seem ridiculous by trying to do too well but I do know that I am going to be judged and I must summon up my very best to give a perfect presentation for the sake of my own honour!

Sleigh tandems

In Canada and the USA there is a 200-year tradition of winter tandem driving which is still carried on today at shows and over 'country courses on snow'.

In 1989, in Canada, an article by Lucinda Fisher was published in the *Carriage Journal*, entitled 'Montreal sleighing memories of 1826'. This gave details of the presentation of eleven tandems on top of Mount Royal, the highest peak in Montreal, the 'sleighing capital' of Canada and the site of many Christmas festivities.

> The young officers of the imperial garrison, with their sporting tandem turnouts, liked to show off their finest horses, sleighs and harness bells, and were accompanied by nice girls or ladies wrapped in expensive, superb furs. The smart sleigh was escorted by a groom sitting on a small seat behind and out of hearing of the couple's conversation.

Even though the garrison of Montreal departed in 1870, the tradition of sleigh tandems has been preserved up to present times thanks to the efforts of the Canadian Sleighing Club.

In the mountainous regions of Vermont and New Hampshire in the northern USA, farmers have maintained the tradition of sleigh driving. It was one of their number, named Justin Morgan, who, in 1850, began to breed a very pure strain of horses that proved to be high-stepping trotters rather in the style of Hackneys – a most appropriate action for driving in snow. It is quite common nowadays to see a tandem of Morgans hitched to a sleigh at winter driving shows. In 1992, the Carriage Association of America held a winter meeting in Minnesota which drew almost 100 entries of sleighing turnouts pulled by singles, pairs, four-in-hand and tandem teams.

Tandem sleigh in a painting by O. Eerelman, 1904. (With kind permission of the National Carriage Museum, Leek, the Netherlands. Photo by John Stoel)

In northern Europe superb sleighing events are held in Scandinavia and also in the Netherlands where there are many old accounts of tandems put to sleighs, especially in E.A.L. Quadekker's *Book of the Horse*: 'Driving a tandem before a sleigh can be seen and it is very pleasant to do and it has the great advantage of giving the riding or driving horse some exercise in the winter out on the snow or ice.' It is a tradition that is still well maintained today by the Netherlands tandem clubs.

In Switzerland, beautiful sleigh turnouts are driven in the Grisons, pulled by strong Swiss cobs. On special occasions elegant sleighs from private collections in Basle and Zurich are shown in public and the Swiss Tandem Club likes to show tandem horses put to sleighs.

Disabled drivers

Following the end of the Second World War, I began to practise orthopaedic surgery. At that time this was a very new branch of medicine which had been brought to France by British and American surgeons dealing with the casualties of war.

By 1986, with some emotion, I was witness to the abilities of young handicapped drivers at the Windsor World Driving Championship, but none of them was able to drive tandem. In 1993, a 30-year-old Frenchman who was totally paralysed in both legs after an accident, showed his pugnacity and skill in sailing alone from France to La Martinique. It is my profound hope that tandem driving, which is a very difficult discipline but which holds great interest for young men and women like the above-mentioned sailor, will be made possible for them by courtesy of a special seat constructed through the joint efforts of specialists in the field of sport tandem driving and orthopaedic surgery.

Other British tandem competitions

The combined driving event is judged under FEI regulations.

Some shows have driving competitions against the clock, which are not very suitable for a tandem class. These are often tandem ride and drive classes, where a changeover from harness to saddle and back again is completed in seconds. The two harness sections are driven in tandem over an obstacle course with seconds added for markers displaced. In the ridden section, the leader is ridden round a show jumping course and seconds are added for any jumps that are knocked down.

Non-competitive meets and drives are also held during the summer months by the British Driving Society for those people who like to meet up with other tandem enthusiasts but who do not wish to compete. Each spring, the BDS Journal publishes all the latest news of past events and gives the programme for the new season.

I was invited to the annual tandem meeting organised by the BDS in 1989. This was held in Kent on a bright, hot, sunny day in summer. I remember noticing the following points with great pleasure and approval:
- No tandem team, neither horses nor ponies, was wearing ear bonnets.
- No tandem leader was put to tandem bars.
- No tandem team was put to a four-wheeled carriage.
- No one was driving two-handed.

17

Tandem dressage, high school and higher equitation

Dressage to music

The test takes place in an arena of 100 × 40 m (109 × 44 yd). The three judges sit at C, B and E. From salute to salute, the test must not exceed seven minutes.

Each presentation must include extended and collected trot and a walk of no less than 40 m (44 yd). Backing is permitted but not compulsory. Canter and gallop are allowed. All of the rest of the programme is up to the driver. A groom or passenger must be carried in the carriage. The horses, legs may be bandaged if wished. The driver should provide his or her own musical cassette, which will be played when the carriage enters the arena.

Scoring

As in classic dressage, 50 points are allocated:
- For technique and the horses' way of going – 10 points. This covers: gaits – ground covered by each pace – impulsion – bending – rhythm – transitions – immobility at halt.
- Execution of the figures and harmony of the programme – 10 points. This covers the harmony of the paces, change of direction of the horses, a well-designed course and good use of the arena.
- The presentation of special movements – 10 points. Special movements must be innovative, reasonable and in keeping with the horses' abilities and way of going. If they are not, the driver will lose marks instead of winning more.
- It is permitted to change tempo in time with the music – 10 points. This means that the horses may change their tempo when the music does.
- General impression – 10 points. This covers the presentation of the entire equipage at one glance. What has caught the judges' eye? Has it been a good show?

Judging dressage to music

Even in 1993, many judges had not really become accustomed to judging musical dressage. The most difficult thing involved is to follow the route taken by the equipage without having the slightest idea what will happen at the next corner. When judging such a performance, I would very much like to have at my disposal a short list of the movements which I shall have to give my opinion on, especially the presentation of special movements. Without this some judges may perhaps end up awarding points more on the general overall impression rather than the exact judging of each of the five categories of scoring during the seven minutes.

Tempo
The special movements must be performed with good impulsion and in keeping with the stride of the horses. It is best to begin with a walk of 40 m (44 yd), halting to salute and then continuing at the trot, changing the paces and the tempo in time with the music, which can look very stylish if your horses are clever enough to follow the beat of the music with their own rhythm.

Special movements
You must combine imagination and a good choice of music with a sensible appreciation of the standard of dressage that your horses are capable of.

After the salute and walk, do not stop or go too deep into the corner. Instead, choose a very open serpentine down the centre line, AXC, possibly driven with one hand. Avoid difficult movements which will break the tempo. It is better to work the merry-go-round. The snailshell can begin at canter, come back to trot, then to walk and finish with the canter of both horses or only the leader.

In 1993, Mrs C. Bush, a young English friend of mine, was clever enough to present her distinguished leader trotting in shoulder-in along the long side of the arena while the wheeler followed in a straight line along the boards.

It is strictly forbidden in classic dressage to change the tempo of the trot but, here, changes of tempo are permitted if in time with the music and will create a most stylish presentation if done well.

The opinion of Major Coombs
- 'There is plenty of good music available in strict trot tempo and recent technology has also produced a sophisticated amplifying system which enables it to be played faster or slower without any effect on its pitch or tone.'
- 'There is no prohibition on judges displaying their marks at the end of each test in order to add to spectator interest.'
- 'In the foreseeable future, it is not inconceivable to contemplate the possibility of free tests to music replacing the existing standard tests for Competition A of trials and thereby increasing their appeal to spectators and the artistic ingenuity demanded of competitors.'

In conclusion
It is my own opinion that horses and ponies are natural music lovers, as can be seen at military shows where they spontaneously adopt a good rhythm when they hear familiar tunes. Thus, on hearing the trumpets from *Cavalleria Rusticana*, the famous opera by Pietro Mascagni (1890), they will begin to trot proudly, spontaneously producing a more elevated trot or even a self-dictated passage.

'Music is, I think, the least disagreeable of noises' (Samuel Johnson, 1750). Let tandem driving take full advantage of it!

Tandem equitation

Preliminary equitation of the leader and wheeler under saddle

Tjeerd Velstra of Deurne High School in the Netherlands maintains that the essential part of the preparation of tandem dressage horses is to ride each of them in *basse école* to the standard of category M of the National German Federation, which corresponds to category B of the National French Federation.

Basse Ecole ridden dressage categories

German Fed.	English	French Fed.
S/Schwer	Advanced	A/Haute Ecole
M/Mitte	Medium	B/Moyen
L/Leicht	Novice	C/Facile
A/Anfanger	Preliminary	D/Débutant

The standard required at ridden M category calls for work on two tracks: shoulder-in, diagonal-across, neck to the wall (*travers*), croup to the wall (*renvers*) – which represents a high standard of dressage which, I imagine, must seldom be attained by drivers in France and Britain when compared with drivers from the Netherlands, Germany and Switzerland.

Mounted tandems

Tandem riding is not something that is done for fun or simply once, 'to see what it feels like', during winter training. Mounted tandems have a long tradition. I have a

Showing youngstock at the Moritzburg stud, East Germany 1975.

photograph, taken at the German stud farm of Moritzburg in 1975, showing the Arab brood mare Galib el Afas in canter behind her yearling leader who is not precisely in line but makes an attractive picture as he trots earnestly along watched over closely by Mummy and their 'driver'. Such mounted tandems are a particularly popular way of showing yearlings at sales in the Netherlands and Belgian Flanders.

Tandem high school riding

Over six consecutive years during the 1950s, Colonel Margot, *écuyer en chef* of the Cadre Noir, Saumur's high school, presented a *reprise de dressage* of twelve mounted tandems ridden by officers in pure, academic style.

Today, Colonel Poirier from La Garde Republicane presents a wonderful show of light, mounted tandems ridden by junior officers. This presentation was first given at the Montreal World Fair in 1967. The way in which the reins are held is particularly interesting. The left hand of the rider holds the four reins of the full-bridled mounted horse as a military rider was accustomed to do in the past in order to free the right hand to carry a sword or lance. The long left rein of the leader is held over the upper rein of the mounted horse and the leader's right rein is held by the right hand alone. At the beginning of training, in order to create the necessary impulsion in the leader, the rider also holds a whip or long stick in his right hand. As well as generating impulsion, the use of this stick or whip also gives a rein aid on the right side of the leader's croup.

La Garde Republicaine.

Later on, although the rider has dispensed with the whip, the same movement of the right rein on the leader's croup will produce the required impulsion thanks to the conditioned reflex that has now been taught to the horse.

The dressage test ridden by the junior officers is performed in a small manège. It asks for variations in the tempo of trot and canter and the plan of movements is very classical: serpentine, a figure of eight, snailshell, wings of the windmill – all executed in complete silence without any sound at all save, from time to time, the chink of passing stirrup irons. It is a very original and impressive tandem display indeed!

(This presentation is given, free of charge, every first Thursday of the month in the riding school of la Garde Republicaine Barracks, boulevard Henri IV, Paris.)

In the circus

During the time of Napoleon III and Queen Victoria, mounted tandem dressage was very fashionable in circus entertainment. Set to music, wonderfully elegant grey horses were presented mounted by a rider in a white tail coat with silk lapels or ridden side saddle by a lady in a long dress that nearly touched the ground.

In 1970, in her family circus in Munich, Christel Sembach-Krone showed her two stallions, Toledo, an Andalusian, who was under saddle, and Conversano Almerina, a Lipizzaner, as leader, in the traditional, very small circus ring. She rode collected canter, with both horses changing legs together – 1-2-3-4 change, 1-2-3-4 change, 1-2-3-4 change ...

The greatest difficulty is found in reducing the number of strides to one, thus producing a change at every stride.

Christel Sembach-Krone, Munich 1971. (Photo copyright Gotfried Schmidt)

In French this is known as *changement au temps*; in English it is called one-time flying change. As far as I am aware, Christel is the only rider who has ever been able to achieve this with a mounted tandem team. She begins with flying change of the two horses together – left and right and left and right, etc. – for two or three circuits of the ring. Then she asks for flying change by the leader to the left and the mounted horse to the right, and vice versa, which could be called 'tandem cross flying change canter', all the way round the ring again. It is a most spectacular and unequalled display!

Equestrian tact and sensitivity of touch

According to the *Collins English Dictionary*, the archaic meaning of the word 'tact' is a sense of touch. It also means a sense of what is fitting and skill or judgement in handling delicate situations.

An acute sense of touch enables us to analyse the fragility of an object and to assess the amount of strength with which to hold it. Thus we can pick up an egg or a crystal wine glass without breaking them or hit a golfball with maximum force.

In human beings the areas of greatest sensitivity to touch are the fingertips, lips and tongue. In horses, they are the feet, lips and tongue.

The tact of the driver

It is the tension of the reins which transmits the feel of the driver's fingers to the lips and tongue of the horse. This contact forms a unique bond between the human and the horse or, even more astonishingly, between a tandem driver and two horses in line.

It is the quality of the contact given by the driver through his or her harmonious handling of the reins, with fingers, wrists, elbows and shoulders acting like a series of shock absorbers along the way, that determines the feel that is received by the mouths of the horses.

The tandem horses receive pressure from the reins on the bit which acts on the mucous membrane of the lips and tongue. If the rein handling is flexible enough, the horses will accept the contact happily, mouthing their bits and salivating enough to produce a small amount of creamy froth at the corners of their mouths.

Lightness

The suppleness of good rein handling will produce a similar supple reaction in the horse's muscles so that it is able to propel the considerable mass of its body forward without straining or cramping.

Conclusion

The term 'equestrian tact' is used to describe the sensitivity and subtlety of feel that must exist between the driver's hand and the horses' mouths. A good quality contact will produce harmony, calmness and lightness in your tandem team. Without 'equestrian tact', your contact is certain to become a two-way exchange of tightness, cramping and pulling – at which point your tandem team will either stop dead or gallop off to hell with you!

No foot, no horse!

This is an old horseman's saying that is still commonly quoted in Britain. It is certainly true that if the horse's feet are not good, the horse will constantly be clumsy, stumble, go badly or even be lame. In this way, the quality of the foot actually dictates the quality of the horse.

The horse's foot

Just as a person can feel their way along in the pitch dark through the touch of their own shod feet, so a horse is able to balance its massive body on four comparatively slender limbs thanks to the sensations received through its feet when they touch the surface of the ground. Throughout all the manoeuvres a horse is called upon to undertake – walking along a road, cantering across country, jumping fences or being driven in tandem – it is the feet which provide the horse with its sense of balance.

As the horse walks along, a widespread system of

extremely sensitive nerves records the exact pressure produced by the contact of each foot with the ground. In this way these billions of tiny sensors are able to test the ground and pass back such vital information to the horse's brain.

The brain as a computer
The information transmitted to the horse's brain via the body's nervous system relates to very specific areas of the brain and its functions and senses. Information received via the eyes will have an effect on where the horse places its feet – hence the French saying 'good foot, good eye', meaning that the horse that does not stumble or trip, but keeps its balance over all kinds of terrain, must have excellent eyesight.

A keen sense of hearing enables the horse to maintain its equilibrium in the same way as, in people, the sense of hearing is allied to the sense of balance.

Every piece of information received by the horse's senses of touch, hearing, smell and sight is analysed by the horse's brain – the 'computer' which controls the muscles and the motor nervous system – to prepare the horse for movement and to dictate speed and tempo.

The ancient horse
About 55 million years ago the ancient ancestor of the horse first appeared on this planet. This animal had a three-toed foot which evolved over millions of years into a one-hooved foot which was better adapted for fleeing from predators.

When, 3,000 years ago, man first began to domesticate the horse, he realised very early on that the horse's skill, stamina and stability depended on the quality of its feet. Nowadays, thanks to genetic selection, good breeding programmes and the skills of modern farriery, the horse's foot is perfectly suited to fulfil the requirements of classical dressage riding and competitive riding and driving, so that now we can also say, 'good blood, good foot!'.

The tempo of a tandem team
When two horses are trotting side by side they may come to match their steps because of the sensitive understanding that exists between them. 'The horse which moves less freely in a pair will almost always make strenuous efforts to match the stride of his better moving partner, until they get to a synchronic tempo' (T. Coombs).

Such a sympathetic understanding is much more difficult to achieve in a tandem team because the leader is always far out in front of the hard-working wheeler which is pulling the carriage alone. Even when the technique and precision of the driver's hand are excellent, matching the paces calls for very sensitive, well-bred horses. Synchronised tempo will only become possible if the vibration of the leader's footfalls are transmitted, via the brain and nervous system of the wheeler, to the feet of the wheeler, and vice versa. Only after intensive, strict training will you see the best tandem teams trotting 'in step' throughout the movements of dressage tests.

Free tandem to music
To produce a tandem turnout that shows the best harmony in matching the paces of the two horses to the tempo of the music, you must seek to synchronise the three tempos of the leader's foot, the wheeler's foot and the beat and

Matching stride. Hamburg 1991.

rhythm of the music. The charm of tandem dressage to music lies in changes of tempo in the music that are concurrent with simultaneous changes of tempo by both leader and wheeler. Thus, 'no foot, no horse, no tandem dressage to music!'.

A last word

The German National Equestrian Federation publishes a booklet on winter schooling, drawn largely from work done in the preparation of carriage horses in Warendorf. This booklet suggests a programme of progressive difficulty through the practice of eight single- and pair-driving lessons and six four-in-hand and tandem driving lessons. Schooling is done in a 80 × 40 m (87 × 44 yd) manège and independent dressage tests are practised, which are different from the FEI tandem dressage tests. Many good ideas for free tandem dressage to music will be found in these independent tests.

18
Final notes

- In the last 20 years, thanks to the efforts of HRH Prince Philip, four-in-hand events have become very popular.
 In the last ten years, it seems that tandem drivers who take part in three-day events represent only about half of the drivers on the European continent and less than a quarter of those in Britain.
- In 1990 Switzerland seemed to have become the leader of tandem driving in Europe, and it was the Swiss Tandem Club which organised the first competition for the Swiss Tandem Cup in 1992. However, although all the tandem drivers who competed took part with pleasure in the dressage and obstacle competition and showed much skill, about half of them did not wish to compete in the marathon. For this reason, the vice president of the club created two categories, one without a marathon and one with a marathon. In this way, drivers in each category were able to compete for the substantial prizes donated by the sponsors who supported the event.
- France has few tandem enthusiasts at present but their numbers increase yearly and a 1992 survey by 'Association Française d'Attelage shows that about a quarter of their members drive tandem, mostly for fun and at weekends.
- Germany has many more tandem drivers. A Hamburg Tandem Drive has been held each year since 1988. This takes place in mid October, which also allows the four-in-hand specialists to come and show what they can do with a 'single tandem instead of two tandems side by side'. One very wet day, I saw 26 tandems of horses and D and C ponies and four randems competing in the dressage and obstacles tests. Had the weather been fine, nearly 50 tandems would have attended.
- In the Netherlands three tandem club's have been established since 1993. Their membership is made up of well-known Dutch drivers.
- International championships are currently not open to tandems, but it has been suggested that 'world championships should be contested by national teams, each consisting of a four-in-hand, a pair, a tandem and a single turnout and some suggest a national team should consist of ponies as well as horses in each category' (T. Coombs).
- In Canada, the USA, Australia and New Zealand tandem driving has been popular for many years and local competitions are becoming more and more common.

A two-day event in France

With the help of his most charming and efficient wife, Paul de Brantes, a very experienced international French

Dufferin Majorette and Dufferin Temptress driven by Thomas Ryder, Devon 1964.

judge, has held a tandem driving weekend at Chateau de Chitenay in the Loire countryside since 1993.
- Saturday morning – tandem presentation
- Saturday afternoon – tandem to music
- Sunday morning – 'tandem country course'
- Sunday afternoon – tandem obstacle driving

This excellent idea of a 'country course' is much better suited to traditional tandem equipages than a cross country or a marathon.

Suggested rules for a 'tandem country course'
- The same traditional vehicle will be used throughout the competition.
- The country course will be free of dangerous areas and will permit an old, tan-varnished tandem cart to complete the course without a scratch on the paint or endangering the lamps.
- The distance will be approximately 8 km (5 miles) to be covered at a free pace.
- The average speed shall be: horses 16 kph (10 mph); ponies 14 kph (nearly 9 mph).
- Foreign competitors shall receive financial help with expenses.
- There will be generous prizes.

The proposed obstacles on the country course
1. Halt before the wrought-iron gates of the chateau, which must be opened by the groom. The tandem drives through and the groom then closes the gates. The groom must sit in the carriage when entering or leaving the obstacle zone.
2. After entering the obstacle zone, both driver and groom must dismount from the carriage. The leader's reins and traces must be untied and then the groom leads the leader off and around a tree about 30 m (33 yd) away as quickly as possible. The leader is then put to again and the carriage leaves the zone. Apart from at very specific obstacles which require the groom to descend from the carriage, he or she must always remain on board.
3. There will be an open tandem slalom in a meadow, through artificial gates with dislodgeable markers.
Time: 0.5 penalty point for each second behind the time and 5 penalty points for each mistake when going through the obstacles.

Leopold Rothkirch, President of the German Riding and Driving Association, was the presiding judge. He advocated this 'English style' of tandem competition be adopted on the European continent and throughout the tandem world as a way of retaining the high quality of this very special form of driving. 'We look forward to such well-organised tandem weekends in the future for the mutual enjoyment of the horses, ponies, competitors and public. It is our hope for the future.'

In conclusion
- Tandem driving is a modern sport – a high percentage of tandem drivers consider tandem driving to be a sport and love to compete in marathons.
- Tandem driving is an art – a high percentage of tandem drivers consider tandem driving to be an art that is significant for its charm, quality, entertainment, appeal, and pleasure – no English reins, no accomplished tandem driver!
- Finally, my friend Tom Coombs says: 'Horsemanship is partnership.'

I say: 'Tandemship is leadership!'

The tandem driver's nightmare. (Gray–Parker 1900)

Bibliography

Achenbach, B. von, *Anspannen und Fahren*, Berlin, 1925

Adams, O.R., *Lameness in Horses*, Lea and Febiger, Philadelphia, 1974

An Old Guard, *The Coach Horn and the Tandem Horn*, Köhler and Sons, 185 Picadilly, London, 1801

Benoit, E. and Goeltzer, H., *Nouveau Dictionnaire Latin-Français*, Lib. Garnier et Flammarion, Paris, llè édition

Berkebile, Don H., *American Carriages, Sleighs, Sulkies*, Dover, New York, 1977

British Driving Society, Annual Journals, Barford, Warwick, GB

Cazier Charpentier, H., *L'Attelage Moderne*, Lib. Mézières, Paris, 1975

Manuel d'instruction d'Attelage, Lavauzelle, Paris, 1984

Comminges, Comte de, *Dressage et Manège*, Plon, Paris, 1897

Coombs, Major T., *Horse Driving Trials*, David and Charles, Newton Abbot, 1985

Horsemanship, The Crowood Press, Swindon, Wilts., 1991

Crafty (Victor Geruzez), *Paris à Cheval, Paris au Bois, La Province à Cheval*, Plon, Nourrit and Co., Paris, 1886

Dauzat, A., *Nouveau Dictionnaire Etymologique*, Larousse, Paris, 1968

Decarpentry, General, *Equitation Academique*, Hazan, Paris, 1949; English edn, *Academic Equitation*, J.A. Allen, 1971

Diepold, B. de, *A L'Ecole de L'Attelage*, Maloine, Paris, 1988

Edimbourg, S.A.R. P. d', *L'Attelage de Competition*, Lavauzelle, Paris, 1984

Finbert, Elian-J, *Chevaux*, Margueritat, Lausanne, 1962

Gerurez, Victor (see Crafty)

Guérinière, F. R. de la, *Ecole de Cavalerie*, 1733, new edition Chastruss et Co, Brive, 1969; English edn, *School of Horsemanship*, J.A. Allen, 1994

Hekimian, E., *Le Comportement du Cheval*, Crépin Leblond, Paris, 1973

Hinrichs, R., *Tänzer an Leichter Hand*, Verlag W. Schröer, 1989

Histoire de la Locomotion/Terrestre, L'Illustration, Paris, 1936

Hontang, M., *Psychologie du Cheval*, Payot, Paris, 1954

Howlett, E., *Driving Lessons*, Charles Schlaeber, Paris, 1906

Larousse Encyclopedique, Larousse, Paris, 1960

Léné, Sellier harnacheur, *La Sellerie Française*, Brice Thomas, 1878

Lepouriel, V., *Procédés Pour Developper le Tact Equestre*, Cheval et Pédagogie, Saumur, 1991

Leslie, Anita, *Jennie: the Mother of Winston Churchill*. Hutchinson, London, 1969; reissued George Mann, Maidstone, 1992

Littré Dictionnaire, Gallimard-Hachette, Paris, 1951

Mauleon, Marquis de, *Methode de Dressage, Travail entre les Guides*, Deladoure-Privat, Toulouse, 1897

Montigny, Comte de, *Piqueurs, Cochers, Grooms*, Librairie Militaire, Paris, 1865

Morley Knight, Captain C., *Hints on Driving*, J.A. Allen, 1884, 1894, 1905, 1969, 1973, 1991

Nissen, J., *Horses*, Burke, USA

Onions, C.T., *Oxford Dictionary of English Etymology*, OUP, 1966

Pape, Max, *Die Kunst des Fahrens*, W. Keller G., Stuttgart, 1966

Podhajsky, A., *L'Equitation*, Nymphenburger Verlag, Munich, 1965

Quadekker, E.A.L., *Het Paardenboek*, Holland, 1880

Saurel, E., *Le Cheval*, Larousse, 1966

Schoenbeck, R., *Deutsche Fahrkunde*, 1900 edition

Schwark, H.J., *Pferdezucht*, VEB Deutscher Land Verlag, 1900 edition

Seunig, W., *Am Pulsschlag der Reitkunst*, E. Hoffman Verlag, Heidenheimer, 1961

Sidney, S., *The Book of the Horse: Gallops and Gossips*, Cassel, London, 1874, 1893

Silver and Haddlesey V., *Chevaux de Haddlesey*, Sun, Paris, 1978

Soler, L., *Historia del Coche*, Ciguena, Madrid, 1952

Steinbrecht, Gustav, *Das Gymnasium des Pferdes*, 1865; French edn *Le Gymnase du Cheval*, Epiac, Paris, 1963

Thelwell, N., *Riding Academy*. Methuen, London, 1985

Velstra, T., *Manuel du Cheval d'Attelage Moderne*, Iska Verlag AG, Weggis (Switzerland), 1988

Walrond, S., *A Guide to Driving Horses*, Nelson, 1971
Encyclopedia of Carriage Driving, J.A. Allen, London, 1974, 1979, 1988
Looking at Carriages, J.A. Allen, London, 1980, 1992
Fundamentals of Private Driving, British Driving Society, 1969
Driving a Harness Horse, J.A. Allen, London, 1992

Webster's Unabridged Dictionary of English Language, Delithium Press Ltd, USA, 1989

Wille, Dr J., *Benno Von Achenbach*, Iska Verlag A.G., Weggis, 1991

Wrangel, Graf C.G., *Das Buch von Pferde*, Schickhardt and Ebner, Stuttgart, 1888

Youatt W., *The Horse, and a Dissertation on the American Trotting Horse*, Lea and Blanchard, Philadelphia, 1845

INDEX

Page numbers in *italics* refer to illustrations

Achenbach, Benno von *88*, 89
Achenbach method of long-reining 53
American check-reins 5
American trotting horse 7
ancient horse 142
apron 128, 130
Association Française d'Attelage 144

back band 23
Basque-Navarre pony 14
basse école ridden dressage 138
bearing reins 21–2
bell 25
bending 41, 46
Bill Vine full hand 83–4, 103
billets 20, 24
bit 20–2, 111
    American upper 6
    Buxton 20–1
    curb 111
    elbow 21
    Fulmer 40
    Liverpool 21
    snaffle 21, 40, 111
blinkers 20, 27, 111

box seat 110–11
brain of horse 142
bridge obstacle 123, 125
bridle 20, 22, 23, 111

cabriolet 18
Cambridge University 1
carriage 19, 90, 123
cart
    English 17
    four-wheeled 19
cavesson, lungeing 40–1
changement au temps 140
changing direction 65–6
changing rein 106
cheekpiece 20
circling
    dressage tests 102–5
    driving 73
    half-length lunge 46, 47–9, 50–1
circulation 10–11
circus tradition 31, 140
clothing 128, 130
cock fighting 18
cocking cart *17*, 18–19
collar 22, 111
collection 41
combined driving event 135
Competition C 122, 123

circuit 124
obstacles *122*, 123, 124
time 124, 126
track width 123
training 124–5
conditioned reflex 30
cones *122*, 123, 124, 125
corners 49–50, 51
coronary plexus *12*
coronet 11, *12*
country course 146
coup de savate 97
cramping, muscular 49–50
Crimean War (1853-6) 4

dead stop 49
dialogue between driver and team 30–2, 44
disabled drivers 135
dog cart 16–18
Doyle's Patent Safety Rail 16
dressage 19, 55, 73, 101
    basse école ridden 138
    changing rein 106
    circles 102–3
    competition rules 108
    double circle 104–5
    English rein handling 78
    extended trot across diagonal 105

five-loop serpentine 103
halt 105
horses 5
judges 108
quarter circle to left when passing through corners 102
rein back 105–6
ridden test 140
rules for competitions 108
schooling on the lunge 39
Test 3 *101*, 102–6, *107*
to music 136
transition of pace 106
turning circle one-handed 85–6
two-handed driving 78
walk 106
driver 33, 128
    dialogue with team 30–2, 44
    safety harness 111
    tact 141
drives, non-competitive 135
driving
    changing direction 65–6
    circles 73
    competition 125–7
    contact with horses' mouths 69–70
    extended trot 99
    famous drivers 86–7, *88*, 89
    on flat 74

Index

high-seat 18–19
hills 74, 115
lateral flexion on road 66
one-handed 83, *84*, 85–7, *88*, 89, 103
paces 73–4
random 90, *91*, 92–3
revival 4
on road 73–4
single horse 99
to music 8, 142–3
trials 10, 58
video simulator 76
see also English tandem driving; FEI driving trials; turning; two-handed driving

ears 31
 covers 24–5
 net 25
English cart 17
English hand 83, *84*
English Harness Trotter 7
English reins 24, 66
 comparison with two-handed driving 82
 dressage trials 78
 holding 60–1, 62–4
 practising handling 76
 right-angled turn 66
English tandem driving 59–60
equipage 128
equitation 138

fault competition 126
Fechner-Weber law 31
feet 10, 11–12, 141–3
FEI driving trials 94, 109
 Competition B 109–21
 Competition C 122–7
 dressage Competition A 95
 gaits 95–101
 geometry of figures 95
 marathon 109–21
 obstacles 122–7
 presentation 94
Fell ponies 10
fingers 29, 42–3
flexion 41, 46
 lateral 46, 47, 49, 52, 66
 schooling ridden horse 55, 56
flying change, one-time 140
France, two-day event 144–6
French full hand 83, *84*
French saddle 23

gait
 FEI driving trials 95–101
 marathon 113
 matching 142, *143*
 transition 106
gate 113–19
Germany 144
gigs 18, 19
girth 41
gloves 74
grip 29
groom 28
 marathon course 119, 121
 random driving 92
 seat 18
 showing 130–1

Haflingers 15
half-halt *48*, 49
halt *48*, 49, 105
halters 27
hame 22
hands 63–4
 changing direction 65
 driving through a turn 73
 holding reins 61–2, 79
 one-handed driving 83, *84*, 85–6
 right-angled turn 67, 68
 schooling ridden horse 55
 two-handed driving 79, 82
harness 20
 accessories 24–6
 English *21*, 24
 leader 23–4
 maintenance 24
 marathon 111
 nylon 111
 random driving 90
 storage 24
 traditional English 20, 24
 wheeler 22–3
headpiece 20
hearing 30–2, 142
heavy draught horses 1, *2*
hills 74, 115
horn 25–6, 129
horses
 lateral flexion on road 66
 longevity 7
 name 31
 pairs 5
Howlett, Edwin 86–7
hunting
 dog cart 17
 tandem 133
Hyde Park annual meet 4

impulsion 41, 45, 106

judges, dressage 108

King of Portugal's stud 8

La Garde Republicane 139, 140
lamps 25
language 31
lead bar 111–12
leader 1, 5
 bending 41
 collar 111
 control 59
 harness 23–4
 pulling 118
 putting to 28
 random driving 90
 striking with whip 34
 turning to left 60
 unharnessing 28
 whip cracking 45
legs, schooling ridden horse 55
Level Balance 16
Lipizzaners 8, *9*
long-rein training 52, 53
 combined effect of two reins 54–5
 comparison with lungeing 53–4
 driving tandem on foot *54*
lunge line 41
 half-length 41, *42*, 46–51, 53
 holding 42
 long 41–6, 53
 short 41, *50*, 51, 53
lungeing 41
 bending 46
 circling 50–1
 comparison with long-reining 53–4
 on corners 49–50, 51
 dressage whip 47

Index

equipment 40–1
  side reins 44, 46–7, 50–1
  trotting in large circles 44–5
  two-track work 51
  use of hands 49
  voice commands 44
  whip use 43, *44*, 45
Lusitanos 5, 7, 8

marathon 15, 109
  bridle 111
  collars 111
  Competition B 109
  distance 112
  gaits 113
  harness 111
  obstacles section 113–17
  official inspection of course 119, *120*
  penalty zone 113
  rules 109, 112–17
  safety measures 112
  Section A-D 112, 113
  Section E 112, 113–17
  spare equipment 112
  tandem bars 111–12
  time 112
  vehicles 109
  walking the course 119, *120*, *121*
mares, driving 8
martingale 22
meets, non-competitive 135
middle horse 90
Morley Knight, C. 74, 76
mounted tandems 138–40
mounting 28
moving off 28
muscular contraction 49

music 8, 136
  free tandem 142–3

neck flexion 47, 66
needle-bit 40
Netherlands 144
noseband 20

obstacle driving 15
obstacles for Competition C 122–7, 126
  cones *122*, *123*, *124*, *125*
obstacles for country course 146
obstacles for marathon 113–17, *121*
  approaching 118–19
  artificial 114–15
  building training course 118
  dislodgeable elements 114–15
  fixed 121
  hills 115, 118
  natural 115–17
  water 115, 116–17
Okapi 74, *75*, *110*
Oliveira, Nuno 7, 55, 106
overtaking 65–6

passage 8, 96
Pavlovian reflex 30
Phursac 74, *75*, *110*
piaffe 8
pinch 29
plantar cushion 11, 12
pony 13–15
  dynamic efficiency 12
  Grade D 10, 13, 15
  grading standard 10
  tandems 10–15, 132–3
  trials 15

pulleys for rein handling practice 76
pulling, training 118
putting to 27–8

races against the clock 6–7
random driving 90, *91*, 92–3
rear bar 111–12
rein-back 53, 54, 73, 105–6
reins
  Achenbach 89
  adjustment 64, 79
  buckles 77, 78, 79, 86
  centre 64
  clamps 78, 86
  cleaning 24
  contact with horses' mouths 69–70
  crossing 62
  dressage tests 101
  holding 60–1, 79
  lead 24, 61–2, 64, 68, 70, 71–2
  looping 70, 71, 72, 80–1, 82
  lungeing 40, 41
  one-handed driving 83
  random driving 92
  side 41, 46–7, 50–1
  tandem high school riding 139
  twinning 78–9
  wheel 61–2, 64, 68, 70, 71–2
  see also English reins
ridden horse schooling 55–6
ride and drive classes 135
roller, lungeing 41
roller-bar terrets 23
rugs 128

saddle 22–3

safety harness 111
schooling 29
  bending 46
  long-rein training 52–5
  on the lunge 39
  ridden horse 55–6
  single harness 56, *57*, 58
  terminology 29
  winter programme 143
Sembach-Krone, Christel 140
serpentine
  five-loop 103
  obstacles for Competition C 123, 125
showing 128–31
  apron 128, 130
  British classes 131–2
  clothing 128, 130
  groom 130–1
  hunting tandem 133
  lady driver 130
  no groom 131
  passenger 131
  pony tandem equipage 132–3
  presentation 131, 132
  sleigh tandem 133, *134*, 135
  whip 128–9, 130
sight 142
single harness schooling 56, *57*, 58
sleigh tandem 133, *134*, 135
slipper gesture 97
slowing down, prevention 74
spring training 117–19
stallions 5, 8
suicide gig 18
sulky 7
Swiss Tandem Club 144

tact, equestrian 140–1
tandem 1, 2, 3–4
    bars 24, 111–12
    cart 16
    dangers 3, 4
    definition 1
Tandem Club foundation 4
Tandem Club of New York 18
Tandem Club of Woolwich 4, 5, 25
tandem driving *see* driving
tempo of tandem team 142
terrets 22, 23
tethers 27
three-day events 127, 144
three-rein hold 61, 62
time competitions 124, 126–7
trace bearer 23
trace belly straps 24
traces 23–4
    adjustment 96
    long 23–4, 111, 112
    randem driving 90
    repairing 20
tridemists 90
trot 73
    collected 8, 96–7, 98, 99
    diagonal 98
    extended 97–9, 105
    FEI driving trials 95–9
    flying 97
    large circles 44–5
    marathon 113
    mounted 98–9
    in step 100–1, 142, *143*
    working 96
trotters 5–7
tub seat 110–11
turning

corner 68–9
hand position 73
right angle 66–8
turning to left 60, 62, *63*, 65
    acute angle at walk 70–1
    randem driving 92, *93*
    right angle 66–7
    right-hand drive 69
    through gateway 81
    two-handed driving 80
turning to right 62, 63, *64*, 65
    acute angle at walk 71–2
    randem driving 93
    right angle 67–8
    right-hand drive 69
    through gateway 82
    two-handed driving 80
two-handed driving 77
    changing direction 80, 81–2
    hand position 82
    looping reins 80–1, 82
    principles 79–82
    reins 78–9
two-track work 51

U-turn 72
unharnessing 28

vehicles 16–18, 19
    four-wheel 110
    marathon 109–12
    tandem box seat 110–11
    two-wheel 109
    see also carriage
video driving simulator 76
voice commands 28, 30–2
    lungeing 44, 48

walking 73, 106, 113

water obstacles 115, 116, 117–18, 123, 125
weather conditions 74
Welsh ponies 11
wheeler 1, 5
    bending 41, 56
    collar 111
    control 59
    harness 22–3
    pulling 118
    putting to 27
    randem driving 90
    striking with whip 34
    turning to left 60, *63*
    unharnessing 28
    whip cracking 45
whip 28, 32–3
    bastard 37, *38*
    bow-topped 33, 34, 38
    cracking 45, 90, 125
    double thong 33, 34
    dressage 41, 47
    English 32–3, 34, 35, 37, 128–9
    furling 33, 35, *36*
    half-length lunge 47–8
    handling 33–5, *36*, 37
    holding 33, 34
    lash 32–3
    lungeing 41
    maintenance 33
    marathon 112
    putza 37
    randem driving 90
    rotating bow 38
    stick 32
    tandem 41, 42, 43
    thong 32, 33, 34, 35
    use in lungeing 43, *44*, 45

    see also driver
Whitechapel cart 18
Windsor Horse Show (BDS) 132
winter training 116, 117–19
wrist 29, 61, 67, 68, 79, 80

zig-zag obstacles 123, 125